JOURNEYS

CHRIS HEALD

THEMES
for early years

Author Chris Heald
Editor Jane Bishop
Assistant editor Sally Gray
Series designer Lynne Joesbury
Designer Louise Belcher
Illustrations James Alexander
Cover Lynne Joesbury
Action Rhymes, Poems and Stories compiled by Jackie Andrews
Songs compiled by Peter Morrell
Assemblies chapter by Lesley Prior

Designed using Aldus Pagemaker
Processed by Scholastic Ltd, Leamington Spa
Printed in Great Britain by Hartnolls Ltd

Published by Scholastic Ltd, Villiers House, Clarendon Avenue, Leamington Spa, Warwickshire CV32 5PR
© 1996 Scholastic Ltd Text © 1996 Chris Heald
2 3 4 5 6 7 8 9   7 8 9 0 1 2 3 4 5

The publishers gratefully acknowledge permission to reproduce the following copyright material:
© 1996 Clive Barnwell for 'Postcard from the seaside' and 'X it marks the spot'; © 1996 Debbie Campbell for 'Kids in Space' from the musical *First Kids in Space*; © 1996 Gina Douthwaite for 'Up the wooden hill'; © 1996 John Foster for 'Sitting in my bath-tub', 'The double-decker bus' and 'Where are you going Jenny?'; © 1996 Lesley Funge for 'The Steam Train'; © 1996 Jean Gilbert for 'My little car'; © 1995 Carole Henderson-Begg for 'We're going on a journey'; © 1996 Jan Holdstock for 'I wrote a letter to Gran'; © 1996 Jan Jones for 'Feeling the way'; © 1996 Wes Magee for 'The solar system tour' and 'Up the street you go'; © 1996 Tony Mitton for 'Minibeast movements'; © 1996 Catherine Morrell for 'Journeys in your mind'; © 1996 Peter Morrell for 'Where did my banana come from?'; © 1996 Brian Moses for 'Magic carpet ride'; © 1995 Sue Nicholls for 'Go to town Calypso!'; © 1996 Jan Pollard for 'Going places' and 'Travelling'; © 1996 Lesley Prior for assemblies 'Travelling in different ways', 'Taking a journey' and 'Special places'; Scholastic Ltd for an extract from *The Train who was Afraid of the Dark* by Denis Bond © Denis Bond (1992, Hippo Books Ltd); © 1996 Geraldine Taylor for 'Sing to the Swallows'; Transworld Publishers Ltd for an extract from *Emily and the Gold Acorn* by Ian Beck © Ian Beck (1992, Doubleday); Walker Books Ltd for 'Walking through the jungle' from *Walking Through the Jungle* by Julia Lacome © Julia Lacome (1993, Walker Books).
Every effort has been made to trace copyright holders and the publishers apologise for any inadvertent omissions.

British Library Cataloguing-in-Publication Data A catalogue record for this book is available from the British Library.

ISBN 0-590-53461-0

CONTENTS

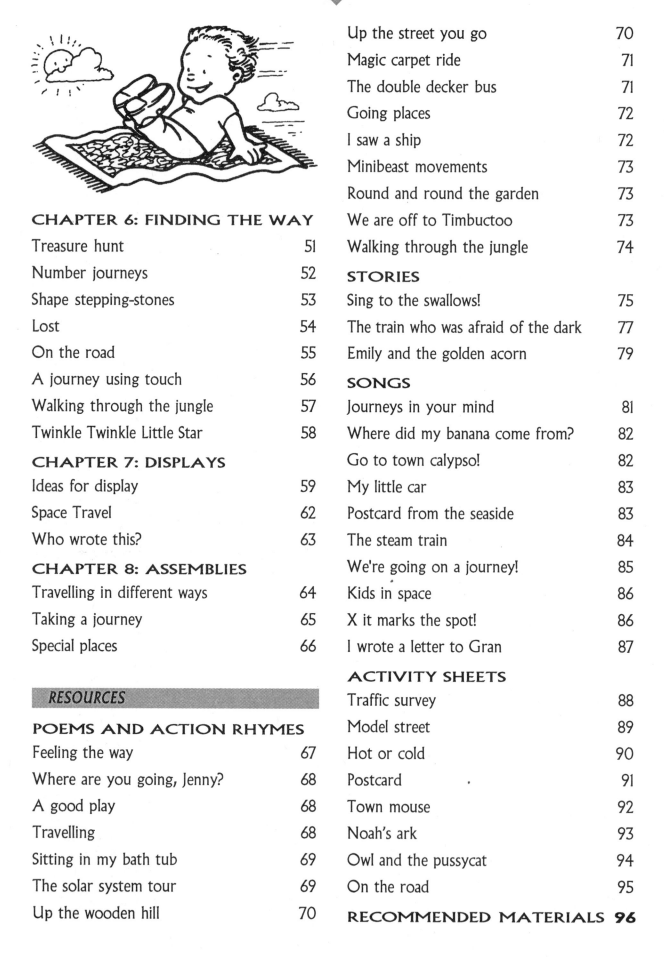

INTRODUCTION

Children today go on lots of journeys. They travel around their own locality by car or public transport. They visit relatives, they go on holiday to foreign countries, sometimes different continents.

In addition, many things in a child's world have journeyed a long way. Food comes from many countries, water comes through pipes and postcards come from holiday destinations right to their homes.

Comfort and security need to be provided for any child before he or she can start to understand or learn about the world. Young children only relate to things which affect them directly; their interest is completely centred on themselves, and it is only by using a topic which relates to their experience that an adult can hope to capture their interest and help them to learn.

CHILDREN'S EXPERIENCES

A topic about journeys harnesses a child's experience. He or she has journeys to talk about and compare with others, real travel experiences they have all encountered. Children will call upon these experiences when playing in the role-play corner, playing with construction toys, or playing with sand and water. They will repeat situations they have encountered on holiday or when going to town, and experiment with reacting in different ways at different times, depending how they feel.

This book aims to provide adults who work with young children with a useful, comprehensive, self-contained package based around the popular Early Years topic of 'Journeys'. The activities have been designed for use with mixed-ability groups of children aged three to six. Each activity is related to an area of the National Curriculum, dealing with the early skills needed by these young children.

The topic is explored from several angles.

Chapter 1 – Our town provides activities based on the local area, journeys made to and from town, knowing addresses, looking at a local map.

Chapter 2 – Holiday journeys considers an imaginary trip to the seaside, asks the children to make their own postcard, and looks at holiday destinations.

Chapter 3 – Stories about journeys centres on well-known tales such as the Town Mouse and the Country Mouse, Noah and his Ark, and the story of the Magi's journey.

Chapter 4 – Moving people invites the children to think about how people in wheelchairs get about, what we do when we visit relatives, and asks the children to think about a journey to move house.

Chapter 5 – Moving objects looks at Father Christmas' journey down the chimney with presents, the journey that water makes to our homes through pipes, and uses water-play to investigate how many plastic animals can be carried in a toy boat.

Chapter 6 – Finding the way explores the feelings of being lost, asks the children to use their sense of touch on a journey and sends them on a Treasure Hunt with picture clues.

HOW TO USE THIS BOOK

Themes for Early Years: Journeys is part of a series of books which have been written for adults who work with young children at home, in playgroups, in nurseries and in Reception classes.

Working with young children is rewarding, interesting and exhausting. The activities undertaken with these children should be stimulating, interesting and appropriate to the age and ability of the children.

Adults who work with young children need to be able to work at the child's level, recognising where experience is limited and always providing what each child needs.

Young children learn best by doing things. They develop their understanding through real experiences such as playing with sand and water, baking and visiting interesting places. They are constantly questioning and need an adult who can provide the answers in ways which they can understand.

The aim of this series of books is to provide adults who work with young children with a comprehensive self-contained package centred around a particular theme.

TOPIC WEB

On pages 8-9 a diagram shows the way activities provided in this book relate to the relevant areas in the National Curriculum. The diagram is called a Topic Web as it enables you to weave together the activities you wish to select to enlarge your children's experience in any particular area. It is a useful aid to planning activities over a period of time, either a week, a month or a term.

THE ACTIVITY PAGES

These pages provide original ideas and others which give a new twist to a familiar idea. Each activity gives a learning objective, group size, what you need, preparation required, what to do, discussion and follow-up ideas. These activities should be used as a recipe — throw in your own special touches and ingredients where you feel it is appropriate for your children.

DISPLAY

General ideas for how to display young children's work are provided. In addition, unique ways of showing work specifically on the Journeys topic are given. Two specific displays are described in detail relating to activities which you may have undertaken from the book.

ASSEMBLIES

This chapter gives suggestions for some specific assemblies or group sharing times based on the theme of Journeys. Each assembly has a practical idea which can involve the children, ways in which you can reflect on the theme and suggestions for a prayer and a song.

RESOURCES

It can take a long time to search out and copy poems, stories and songs on a particular theme. The resources pages in this book provide a selection of action rhymes, poems, stories and songs some of which relate to specific activities and some of which are of more general use.

PHOTOCOPIABLE ACTIVITY SHEETS

Eight worksheets are provided in this chapter each relating to a specific activity in the book. They provide opportunities for the children to work independently although younger children may need adult guidance and assistance.

RECOMMENDED MATERIALS

A book list of useful titles and other resource materials, many of which are mentioned earlier in the book are given on this page.

THEMES
for early years

EXPRESSIVE ARTS

Planning towards the National Curriculum and the Scottish National guidelines 5-14

PREPARING FOR PRIMARY SCHOOL

WHERE TO START

The National Curriculum has been established to make sure that every school in the country teaches the same subjects at all levels. It is intended that any child will be able to go to school anywhere in the country and find the same areas of the curriculum being covered for the same amount of time every week. The subjects covered are: English, Mathematics, Science, History, Geography, Design and Technology, Information Technology, RE, Art, Music and PE.

There is a great deal of learning to be done before starting the work of the National Curriculum. For instance, before children learn to recognise words, they should understand that the written word relates to everyday speech, and they should realise that shapes and colours can be the same or different.

Young children learn best if encouraged to use all their senses in their play. They also need lots of time in free play situations, and certainly should spend much more time playing with selected toys and materials in a free way than working in the traditional school manner.

TOWARDS LEVEL ONE

Children do not start on the National Curriculum until they are five, so the programmes of study were written to suit the maturity of children who have reached their fifth birthday and, depending on where in the country they live, have had

anything from a term to a year in school in a reception class.

The National Curriculum provides a programme of study for each subject, and asks teachers to assess the level of attainment of each child in the country when they reach Year Two, partly by the use of nation-wide tests, but mostly by asking teachers to use their professional judgement to allocate an overall level to each child.

The National Curriculum has not changed the ways that young children learn best. Successful teaching will always start with ascertaining the ability level of the child and work towards the next step in his or her intellectual development.

The Topic Web on pages 8–9 shows how the activities in this book relate to specific areas of the National Curriculum.

THE SCOTTISH NATIONAL CURRICULUM GUIDELINES 5–14

In Scotland, there are National Guidelines for schools on what should be taught to children between the ages of five and fourteen.

These National Guidelines are divided into six main curriculum areas: English Language, Mathematics, Environmental Studies, Expressive Arts, Religious and Moral Education, and finally Personal and Social Development.

Within these main areas, further subjects are found – for example, 'Expressive Arts' includes art and design, drama, music and PE. Strands are also identified within each subject – for example, Mathematics including Problem-solving and enquiry and Shape, position and movement.

Most nurseries will find that the experiences they are offering children will provide a good foundation for this curriculum. The activities in this book have been specially written to prepare for many aspects of it, and they will also fit well into the pre-five curriculum guidelines issued by local authorities throughout Scotland.

We have organised the activities into separate areas of the curriculum on the Topic Web on pages 8–9 to help you with your planning. The children's personal and social development is an ongoing theme that is incorporated throughout the activities in this book.

CHAPTER 1
OUR TOWN

This chapter provides activities to encourage children to explore their local environment including learning home addresses, trips around the town and a look at local maps.

A TRAFFIC SURVEY

Objective

Maths — Handling data and to create a graph.

Group size

Up to ten children.

What you need

Clip-boards, pencils, photocopiable sheet on page 88, large sheets of paper for group graph, paint, felt-tipped pens or crayons, coloured poster-sized paper for backing.

Preparation

Using a black felt-tipped pen, make two graphs. Cut out small pieces of paper to fit on your graphs, so that children can draw pictures of the vehicles they have seen. Photocopy enough copies of the photocopiable sheet 88, one for each child.

If you cannot clearly see a road from your window you will have to take the children to a safe viewing point outside.

What to do

Divide the children into two separate groups for the survey. One group should only tally the types of vehicles going *towards* town / farm / station or any other local feature. The other group should only collect details of vehicles going *away* from this place. Hand out the photocopied sheet, clipboards and pencils.

Every time a vehicle passes, on their side, the children must put a mark on their sheet in the correct box.

When you return to your base, ask each group of children to draw or paint pictures of each vehicle they have seen on to squares of paper which can then be stuck on the graph. The graphs can then be glued onto the large sheet together before they are fixed on to the wall. Add up the totals together and enter the numbers for each vehicle type under each column.

Discussion

Ask the children about the vehicles they have seen. What type of vehicle did they see most? Which did they see least? Where were the vehicles going and why? For example if you saw a fire-engine or a man on a bike with a fishing rod, could you guess where they were going?

Follow-up activities

✧ Sort toy vehicles into lines and count them just like the graph.
✧ If you have an outdoor play area, give the children chalks to draw a roadway to ride along on their bikes. This could be painted over with gloss paint to make a permanent play area designed by the children.
✧ Make up a group story about one of the vehicles you have seen. Where was it going? Who was driving it? What happened next?

I KNOW MY ADDRESS

Objective

English (Speaking and Listening) — To see if the children know their home address.

Group size

A group of ten children.

What you need

Self-adhesive dots in various colours, large sheets of white paper, paint and brushes, string or cord, a map of the area where the children in your group live, an overhead projector (OHP), a blank OHP sheet, OHP pens.

Preparation

Check where the children's homes are on your map. Trace the outline of the relevant streets onto your OHP sheet, trace around the outline on the wall onto your large paper and you will have an enlarged map of the area. If you do not have access to an OHP, you could try to draw a simple enlarged version freehand.

Mix the powder paint ready for use. Put your enlarged map on the wall so that the children can easily reach it.

What to do

Ask the children if they know their home addresses. Explain to them that this means where they live, and that everyone's address is different. If some children can recite their address encourage them to do this. Identify each child's home location on the map. Mark it with a self-adhesive dot. When each child's house has been marked in this way, look at the pattern — do clusters of children live in the same area, or are they all scattered widely?

Ask the children to paint a picture of their house. When these paintings are dry, place them on the wall around the map, with cords stretching from the appropriate dot.

Discussion

Give each child the opportunity to tell their address to the other children. Ask the children if

they know anyone in the group who lives near them — are they able to see the other person's house on the map?

Follow-up activities

✦ Read *The Jolly Postman* by Allan and Janet Ahlberg (Heinemann) and show the children the addresses on the envelopes. Can they think of any other suitable addresses for fairy tale characters?
✦ Set up a writing corner and write cards with each child's address on for them to copy.

A MODEL STREET

Objective

Design and Technology – To make a model street using junk materials and plan a journey around it.

Group size

Up to ten children.

What you need

Shoe-boxes or similar cartons, one for each child, sticky-tape (preferably in a dispenser), adhesive, coloured sticky paper, card of various thicknesses, paper, clear Cellophane, scissors, crayons, felt-tipped pens, wallpaper, a toy bus/ambulance/fire engine or police car, photocopiable activity sheet on page 89, one per child.

Preparation

Take the children on a walk down a nearby street pointing out the different houses and other features. Copy the sheet on page 89, ready for use.

What to do

Use the back of the wallpaper and encourage the children to draw road markings on it to create the street for the houses to be positioned along.

Let them each choose a carton. Explain that they are going to make their carton look like a house or other building. Show them how to cut out opening doors and windows. Demonstrate how to fold paper to make a door which could be stuck onto the carton. Show the children two ways of making windows (a cut out rectangle, and one covered with Cellophane) and a roof (score a piece of card and bend it).

Next let the children begin to make their own individual model buildings. Offer help if it is needed, but encourage the children to try things for themselves.

Once the models are complete, place them along your streets, now let the children choose a vehicle. Put it at one end of the street, then ask one child to choose a house for the car to visit. Ask the child to describe the house, and ask them to push the car to its destination. Make sure that each child gets a turn.

Discussion

Ask the children about the building which they made. What colour is it? What shape is it? What sort of building is it? Which vehicle did they choose? Why? Whose building did they go to?

Follow-up activities

✧ Photocopy the sheet on page 89, and ask the children to draw a road between the two houses.
✧ Can the children draw a map of the street you have made by standing over it and looking at it from above?
✧ Read the poem 'Up the street you go' on page 70 of the resources.

WHERE AM I GOING?

● ●

Objective

English (Speaking and Listening) – To give children the opportunity to guess where people would go by the articles which they are carrying.

Group size

Eight to ten children.

What you need

A comfortable quiet area for your children to be able to sit and listen attentively and speak clearly. Items which will give clues as to destinations for example: library books – library; bucket and spade – seaside; sports bag – sports centre/swimming baths; shopping bag – supermarket; satchel – school; fishing rod – river/lake; ball – park/ football field; suitcase – airport/station.

Choose items which are relevant to your area (in a farming area a bucket might suggest feeding animals rather than the beach!).

Preparation

Hide all the items (behind a screen for example) so that the children will see them for the first time when you bring them out.

What to do

Ask one of the children to stand up and choose one of the articles. Let the child show it to the group, and then ask another child to say where someone might be going if they were carrying it. Give each member of the group a turn to stand up and a turn to answer. Accept all answers, because some children may use a shopping bag to go to the sports centre. However, you can ask questions about an apparently bizarre answer for example a fishing rod *could* be taken to the swimming baths if they run a course on fly-fishing!

Discussion

Which item could be taken to lots of places? (Shopping bag.) Which item could only be taken to one place? (Library book.) Which place do they most enjoy going to? Why? What other things tell you where people are going? What happens when you jingle a dog's leash? (A dog might know it's time for a walk.)

Follow-up activities

✧ Draw some pictures of people carrying something which gives a clue to their destination.
✧ Write the destination under each drawing, and cover it with a flap, to make a guessing game when pinned to the wall.
✧ Draw a simple outline of a bag (see illustration) and photocopy it so each child can decide what it is for – sports bag/shopping bag/handbag/ briefcase etc.

A JOURNEY ROUND THE TOWN

Objective

Physical Education – To take an imaginary journey around the town.

Group size

Up to twenty children.

What you need

A 'lost' item, hats/items for you to wear to represent different people. Suggested characters could be: postman/woman; policeman/woman; shopkeeper; nurse; farmer; footballer/cricketer; vicar/priest.

Preparation

Plan your 'route' clearly in your head, together with a reason for your journey before you involve the children. You could be searching for something lost, or you could be lost and trying to find the way home.

What to do

Start with the children in a group, and explain that they will pretend to go on a journey around town, looking for something which is lost.

Ask for suggestions from the children for what to do. Next don one of the hats and become one of the local characters mentioned above. Encourage the children to ask you - in the role of each character in turn - questions to help find what they have lost. None of these 'people' will have the missing property until the very last one, when the missing item will be found.

Encourage the children to ask the questions they would ask of the real character, and develop any ideas which they have. You may decide that each character has a problem which the children have to solve before they move on. What could help to soothe the vicar's sore throat, so that he can speak to them? What can they do to help the footballer's sore leg?

Discussion

Ask the children about their favourite part of the story. Was it funny or sad? What would you do if you lost something? Who could you ask for help?

Follow-up activities

✧ Use a map to follow the route of your imaginary journey. Can the children draw lines between the places they visited to show where they went?
✧ The children may like to try to illustrate their journey, making a zigzag book and writing 'We went to the...' under each drawing.

HOW DID YOU JOURNEY HERE?

* *

Objective

Maths — To make a graph showing how the children got to your base this morning.

Group size

Eight to ten children.

What you need

Large sheets of white paper, Plasticine in various colours, including flesh shades, PVA adhesive, a small amount of water, spreaders and brushes, a container to mix glue and water, rectangles of lightweight card about 20cm × 15cm, different coloured felt-tipped pens.

Preparation

Join your large sheets of paper together to make one very large sheet. Make a grid ten times the size of your rectangles of card. Write numbers 1 to 10 up the side.

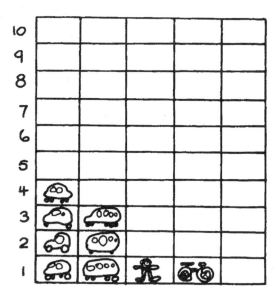

What to do

Give the children a card each and ask them to use coloured Plasticine to make a flat picture on it showing the way they travel to the group each day. Children who journey on foot should make a

picture of themselves, those who travel by car should make a picture of their car using the correct colour, and so on.

When the children have finished their pictures, let them stick their Plasticine to the card with glue.

Next mix a small amount of water with the PVA and show the children how to brush the mixture over their pictures, to form a glaze which will hold the Plasticine together and will give their pictures a glossy finish.

Arrange the pictures on the graph, pointing out the totals for each line. Do some simple sums by counting on from one column to another — how many children came by car and bus for instance.

Discussion

Ask the children about their journey to the group. Do they travel a long way? How long does it take to get here? Does anyone else do the journey every day with them? Do the children ever use different forms of transport from the one they used today?

Follow-up activities

✧ Let the children make their own graphs using one of the data-handling computer-programs available such as GRASS.
✧ Convert the graph into sets by using dolls or model cars. Encourage the children to design and draw their own sets.

MAKING A MAP

Objective

Geography – To make a simple map of an imaginary town.

Group size

Four to six children.

What you need

Large sheets of paper (the reverse side of a roll of wallpaper is useful), A4 sheets of paper, adhesive tape, crayons/felt-tipped pens or thick-tipped marker pens.

Preparation

Talk to the children about what they see on their way to you each day. What would they like to see if they could choose?

What to do

Tell the children that they are going to plan a town for themselves. What should it have in it? Ask the children to draw something they would like in their town on a piece of paper. Suggestions could be swimming baths/a camp site/a fairground/a bandstand and so on.

Let the children decide what hills, streams etc. your town should have, and let them draw these onto your roll of paper accordingly.

Ask the children to cut around their individual drawings and then stick them on their chosen place on the 'map'. Talk about what would be a good place for each item. Would it be best to have a windmill amongst all the houses, or up on the hill where the wind is strong?

Next decide on a name for your imaginary place and write it on the map.

Discussion

What did the children want to have in their imaginary town? Why? What else would they like to have? Is there anything they don't want in their town? Why?

Follow-up activities

✧ Take photographs of some well-known landmarks in your area using a Polaroid camera. Who built them and why? Can the children draw them? Are there any artists in the local area who have painted local scenes?

✧ Go for a walk around your area. What is the place the children like best? What don't they like? Can they do anything about it? (Write a letter to someone who can help to change it.)

COLLECTING THE RUBBISH

• •

Objective

Science — To find out about the journey the dustcart makes around the town.

Group size

A group of six to eight children.

What you need

Disposable plastic gloves for all the children who are going to touch litter, a black plastic sack, self-adhesive labels, felt-tipped pens, a large (A2) sheet of paper.

Preparation

Make a note of the time your rubbish is collected, so that the children can watch it happening. Ring up the council and ask if someone would be prepared to talk to your group about rubbish.

Label your litter-collecting bag with the name of a street close to your base.

What to do

Take out your rubbish with the children when the collectors arrive. Talk about the noises — and the smells! If there is someone to explain the process to the children, ask them about their route around the town, and what happens to the rubbish.

Issue disposable plastic gloves to the children, then take them along your chosen street, putting what you find in the bag. When you return, tell the children to keep the plastic gloves on and look carefully at your findings. Are there any sweet packets? Who do they think dropped those? What about cigarette packets?

Write the name of your street on your large sheet of paper (like a street sign) and then ask the children to stick the litter they found onto the paper. This could then be stuck on the wall with the message: **Did you drop this litter?**

Discussion

Ask the children if they know why we need to have our rubbish taken away. Why don't we just leave it lying around? What would happen if there was no-one to collect it?

Follow-up activities

✧ Put a 'Playmobil' dustcart on the carpet or a table for the children to play with. Include some rubbish for them to pick up (torn pieces of paper).
✧ Write to the local council and ask for a litter-basket in the area where the litter was worst.
✧ Think about different kinds of rubbish. What would a space-man's rubbish be like? A witch's? A king's? A teacher's?

THEMES
for early years

CHAPTER 2
HOLIDAY JOURNEYS

Travel further afield is investigated in this chapter with an imaginary trip to the seaside, writing postcards and a look at holiday destinations.

HOT OR COLD HOLIDAY?

Objective

Geography – To sort suitable clothing to take on a holiday.

Group size

Up to eight children.

What you need

White paper for labels, red and blue felt-tipped pens, two sets of clothes, one set for the beach (bathing costume; sun hat; T-shirt; sandals), the other suitable for a skiing holiday (anorak / *salopettes* or ski-suit; gloves; ski-boots; ski-hat). Two dolls (Sindy / Barbie), one dressed for hot weather and the other one for cold weather, placed next to the corresponding labels to reinforce the concept of hot and cold locations, photocopiable sheet on page 90.

Preparation

Mix all the clothes together in a single pile. Ask the children which colour of felt-tipped pen suits a hot place, and which a cold place, and write the words hot on one label and cold on the other. Copy the photocopiable sheet on page 90, one per child.

What to do

Put the two labels and dressed dolls well apart and explain to the children that they are going to sort the clothes into two sets. Ask them to think about which clothes they would wear if they were going on a holiday either to a very hot place, or a very cold place. Talk about the clothes the dolls are wearing. Ask each child to choose something they would wear to go on holiday with one of the toys, and put it on that pile.

Finally dress two children in the sets of clothes.

Discussion

Why is it important not to get too cold or to stay too long in the sun? What might happen if you get too cold/too hot? Which clothes do the children like best? Which place (hot or cold) would they choose to go to?

Follow-up activities

✧ Ensure the children know how to protect themselves in the sun. Make use of the Australian motto 'Slip slap slop' (Slip on a T-shirt; slap on a hat; slop on some suncream).

✧ Can the children think up a 'slip, slap, slop' saying for cold weather?

✧ Copy the photocopiable sheet on page 90. Ask the children to match the clothes to the correct child. The clothes and children can then be cut out and used as dolls to dress.

✧ Can the children design some clothes for hot or cold weather?

SEND A POSTCARD

• •

Objective

Design and Technology – To design and write a holiday postcard.

Group size

Up to eight children.

What you need

Photocopiable sheet on page 91, white photocopying card, felt-tipped pens, crayons and pencils, examples of holiday postcards (some old ones if possible) with simple messages written clearly on the back.

Preparation

Use the photocopiable sheet on page 91 to provide one blank postcard for each child. Talk about going on holiday and the different types – seaside holidays, farm holidays, ski-ing holidays for example. Ask the children if they have ever sent a postcard. Where did they buy it? Who actually wrote it? Show them the examples of postcards you have brought, and ask them to guess who wrote the message, (parents/friend/grandma/auntie or uncle for example).

What to do

Give each child a blank postcard and explain about the two different sides. Where does the picture go? Where does the writing go? How can you tell?

Ask the children to draw a picture of their favourite holiday destination on the picture side of the postcard.

While the children draw, the adult helpers could do their own card. Encourage the children to try and write a message on their cards. If they are very young children who cannot write yet, encourage them to write marks which have meaning for them.

An adult can help with writing a real address. The cards can then be put on a table for everyone to read, before being taken home (or posted if the cost of postage is available).

Discussion

Who did you send your postcard to? Why? What do you do with the postcards you receive at home? Who would you send postcards to when you were on holiday? What is your favourite sort of picture for a postcard – a sunny place, an animal or the seaside for example?

Follow-up activities

✧ Look at some old postcards people used to send long ago. What is different about them? Look at the people's clothing and the vehicles on the roads.
✧ Talk about the journey the postcard makes. Use video materials available from the GPO about the journey of 'Lenny the Letter', see recommended materials, page 96.

GOING TO THE SEASIDE

Objective

Drama — To experience an imaginary journey to the seaside.

Group size

Up to ten children.

What you need

A clear space large enough for your group to move around freely.

Preparation

Make sure the children are comfortably dressed to allow free movement.

What to do

Say out loud the directions (below) and perform the actions together. Tell the children you're going to the seaside.

Discussion

What did the children like best about the trip? Did anyone feel sick on the bus? What sort of sounds and smells might they notice by the seaside?

Follow-up activities

✧ Ask the children to suggest ideas for going on other journeys. How would they mime travelling on a train?
✧ Provide chalks for the children to draw their imaginary destination.
✧ Say the poem 'The double decker bus' on resources page 71.

Say	Actions
Let's get on the bus	Sit on the floor
It's a bumpy ride	Bounce up and down
The driver blows the horn	Make noise of horn
We're going round a corner	Lean to one side
And another	Lean to the other
We've had to stop for some traffic lights	(Stop bouncing)
And now we're off again	Bounce up and down
(repeat above twice)	
Get off the bus	Stand and walk around your space
And sit on the sand	Sit on the floor
We'll build a sandcastle	Pretend to dig
Put a flag on the top	Stretch up tall
Let's make some sandpies	Sit down
Fill your bucket	Dig and fill bucket
Turn it upside down	Turn and lift bucket
It's a sandpie!	*Repeat last two actions*
Let's make another one	
Let's go for a paddle	
Take your shoes off	Mime taking off shoes
Tip-toe in — it's cold	Tiptoe back and forth
Splash in the water	Stamp feet
Splash your friend	Scoop water with hands
Out of the water and get dry	Rub themselves with hands
Time for a picnic	Mime eating food (sandwiches/crisps/apple)
Let's go for a walk	Walk holding hands
Can anyone find a shell?	Mime picking up
What can you hear?	Cupped hands over ears
Time for an ice-cream	Slurping and licking
Get back on the bus	All sit down

(Repeat the beginning of the journey in reverse)

A TRAVEL AGENTS

Objective

Drama – To perform role play about visiting a travel agents.

Group size

Six in a group.

What you need

A desk / table, toy telephone, typewriter / computer keyboard, chairs, holiday brochures, posters and banners with 'special offers', Blu-Tack, pads of booking forms, rubber stamps and a pad, receipts, paper clips, assorted pens, black felt-tipped pen, livery for the 'staff' (scarves / clip-on badges with names on).

Preparation

Write holiday prices in black felt-tipped pen next to the photographs in the brochures.

Set up the role-play area, sticking posters on the walls and organising it to look as much as possible like a real travel-agents.

Photocopy lots of the booking forms, but do not put them all out at once. Make sure that there are enough for each child to use three or four. A visit to a real travel-agents would be a wonderful stimulus for play and drama if it can be arranged.

What to do

Explain the rules of the travel agents to the children. Two children can be members of staff, the others are customers. Booking forms can be completed – the customer can fill in his or her name, the price of the holiday, and where it is, the travel agent should fill in the date and stamp the booking form when the booking has been finalised with 'head office' over the phone. Everyone should have a turn at doing both things.

Remind the children of the routines of adult behaviour – shaking hands, introducing yourself and thanking people when you are leaving.

Discussion

Ask the children which they preferred, being the customer or being the travel agent? Why? Which was the best holiday in the brochure? Which holiday did most people want to book?

Follow-up activities

◆ Use the postcard photocopiable master on page 91 to make blank postcards for the children to send to their friend from the holiday which they booked at the 'travel agents'.

◆ Ask the children to write and design their own 'special offer' banners and posters, offering cut-price deals on holidays.

WHERE DID YOU GO?

. . . .

Objective

Geography – To study a map of the world and note holiday journeys on it.

Group size

Up to ten children.

What you need

A large map of the world, black cord/thread/ wool, self-adhesive spots, old postcards written from various destinations (brought by the children), light backing paper in a contrasting colour to your cord, a staple-gun and staples, a postcard to you from someone in a foreign country.

Preparation

Put up the backing-paper on the wall and staple the map to the centre of it. Make sure your self-adhesive spots are large enough to stick down the end of your cord in its place on the map. This activity is most effective when it can be added to throughout the summer or even all year. Ask the children to bring in some postcards they have received recently.

What to do

Show the children the map of the world and show them where you live. Then show the children your postcard and show them where this country is on the map – for example Greece. Use a piece of cord to connect the area of Greece shown on the card back to where you live.

Pin the postcard itself up at the side of the map and write the name of the country above it. Add any postcards which the children bring in over a period of time.

Discussion

Whenever a child brings a new postcard to the group, talk about where it is from, and what life may be like there. Is it by the seaside? Is it hot or cold? Are there mountains? What language do the people speak? What sort of food do they eat? Would you like it there?

Follow-up activities

✧ Choose a foreign country. Over a period of a week try some food, wear the costume, listen to the music and learn a few words of the language of that country.
✧ Make a book of the postcards from the most popular country. What can the children find out about it?
✧ Collect souvenirs and pictures from holiday destinations and play a game matching them to their country of origin.

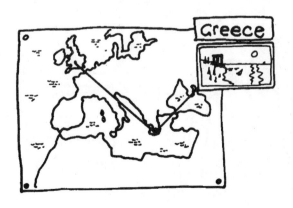

A MUSICAL JOURNEY

Objective

Music – To create the musical effect of a journey.

Group size

Up to ten children.

What you need

Items which will make noises appropriate to a journey. For example: a zip (suitcase), xylophone (going downstairs), wood block (footsteps), whistle (train), hooter (boat), bells (bicycle), silvery chimes – glockenspiel (water), recording of crying seagulls (the seaside), castanets/guitar (Spain), 'Mickey Mouse' voice saying 'Hello everybody' (Disneyland), Bazouki music (Greece).

Preparation

Make sure that each child has something to do. This activity is a group composition and should include every member, whatever their abilities. Decide in advance where your journey is going to take you all.

What to do

Sit the children in a semi-circle and talk about the musical journey you are all going to take. Start at one end of the semi-circle and give the first child the first sound you decide you want to use. If there is no instrument which will make an appropriate sound, ask if any child can make a noise which will fit. Whatever noise they make then represents that part of the journey. This activity could even be done just using voice, if the instruments you need are not available.

The 'journey' could sound something like this:

Adult or child speaks
We packed our suitcases
We were happy
We got into the car
We arrived at the airport
The plane took off
And landed
And we were in Spain.

Sound made
Zip fastener
'Hooray' (voice)
Car horn
Child speaks (holding nose): 'Will passengers for flight six please go to Gate three'
Drum roll
Cymbals
Castanets/guitar/stamping feet.

Discussion

Talk to the children about the instruments they played and why they were appropriate to the parts of the story they represented. Which instrument did they like best? Why? What music do they listen to at home? Can they sing any of it?

Follow-up activities

✧ Play music from other countries and ask the children to draw a picture to show what it makes them think of.
✧ Dress up in the national costume worn in other countries.
✧ Cook some food typical of each country.
✧ Read the poem 'Travelling' on page 68.

PACKING FOR A HOLIDAY

Objective

Maths — To find which is the heaviest suitcase.

Group size

Up to ten children.

What you need

Four suitcases of differing sizes and weights, A3 paper, crayons and pencils, use of a photocopier. Items of varying weights to put in the suitcases, such as suitcase 1 (large case) — empty or one T-shirt (lightest); suitcase 2 (large case) — books and clothes (heaviest); suitcase 3 (small case) — tins of food and clothes (second heaviest); suitcase 4 (small case) — towels (second lightest).

Preparation

Make sure that one of the larger suitcases is empty and lighter than one of the smaller suitcases, so that the children will not put them in order by their size. Try to ensure the two larger and the two smaller suitcases are different colours.

Make a worksheet. Ensure that the suitcases are noticeably different in weight when you pick them up. Make two labels saying 'heaviest' and 'lightest' and put them on the floor with enough space between them for the suitcases to stand.

Place all the suitcases in a jumbled pile somewhere close at hand.

What to do

Ask the children to look at the suitcases and say which one they think is going to be the heaviest and then draw it on their sheet. Now let the children find out if their guesses were right.

Encourage them to put the sign 'heaviest' on the one they found was the heaviest and the sign 'lightest' on the one they found was the lightest. Then let them fill in the part of the sheet which says 'I found out'.

Discussion

Which suitcases looked heavy? Was this right? What was in the heaviest suitcase? Who usually carries your suitcases? How can you help them? What are your suitcases like at home?

Follow-up activities

✧ Make a list of things to put in your suitcases to go on holiday. Can your friends guess where you are going?

✧ Weigh the suitcases to see just how heavy they are. Then weigh the children. Which is the heaviest?

✧ Make a chart of the weights from the heaviest to the lightest.

HOLIDAYS IN THE PAST

Objective

History – To find out what holiday journeys were like for people in the past, compared to our holiday journeys today.

Group size

Up to ten children.

What you need

Photographs of children and adults going on holiday in the late nineteenth and early twentieth century.

Preparation

Find some old photos showing methods of transport that used to take people on holiday.

What to do

Ask the children about their holidays. Show them the old pictures you have found. What are the differences between what the old photos show and what we do on holiday today?

Tell the children that holidays are a new idea in this country for ordinary people. In the past, taking a holiday would have meant not being paid and losing your job and so were impossible. Sundays were the only days for a rest for grown-ups and that is where the word holiday (holy day) comes from. In those days only very rich people had holidays as we know them, ordinary people did not.

Look again at the photos and let the children choose one they like. Ask them to paint their own version of the photo they have chosen. Keep discussing their work as they do it and drawing their attention to details in the photo.

Discussion

Do we wear the same sort of clothes as in the picture these days when we go to the seaside? Why? What can you see in the old photographs that we don't do any more these days? What is still the same today? What sort of transport takes us on holiday today?

Follow-up activities

✧ Make a list of clothes which were worn on holidays in the past. Make a list of modern holiday clothes. What is different? Is anything the same?
✧ Make a collection of old artefacts which children at the beginning of the century would have seen around them.
✧ Look at some paintings at the seaside done at the turn of the century by the Post-Impressionists. Can the children use similar techniques and paint a holiday picture?

CHAPTER 3
STORIES ABOUT JOURNEYS

Journeys in well-known tales provide some interesting opportunities for activities. Stories as varied as Noah and his ark and the Magi's journey start the children off on a variety of work.

THE TOWN MOUSE AND THE COUNTRY MOUSE

Objective

English — To write about the visit of 'the town mouse' and 'the country mouse'.

Group size

Six children.

What you need

Photocopiable sheet on page 92 (one per child), pencils and crayons, a copy of the story *The Town Mouse and the Country Mouse* adapted by Helen Craig (Walker), a packet of green garden canes, adhesive tape.

Preparation

In advance, copy page 92 ready for the children. Use one copy to colour and cut out the figures on the sheet, stick them to card and fix them to the top of two of the canes.

What to do

Read the story, using your cut-out figures on sticks to illustrate it. Repeat, encouraging two children to work the puppets this time, while you read the story for them.

Give each child a copy of the photocopiable sheet. Encourage the children to finish the sentences begun on the sheet in their own words. Help them to sound out any words they want to use, but be prepared to act as scribe. Accept their attempts for what they are — very early or 'emergent' writing.

When the children have finished the writing, they can colour and cut out their mice and make

their own stick-puppets. They can then act out a short puppet-show in pairs.

Discussion

Where would you rather live? In the country or in the town? What is nice about living in a town? What would you hear? What would you see? What is nice about living in the country? What makes it different from the town?

Follow-up activities

✧ Find a piece of recorded music which helps to illustrate the town-mouse's life. For example, the music from 'West Side Story' or 'Barnum'. Let the children listen to it. Then do the same for the country mouse with soothing pastoral music such as Vivaldi or Vaughan Williams.

✧ Ask the children to draw a picture of the inside of either the town-mouse's house or the country-mouse's house. What can they draw that would show everyone whose house it is?

✧ Say the poem 'Where are you going Jenny?' on page 68, substituting 'Mousey' for Jenny!

NOAH'S ARK

Objective

RE – To learn about a story from the Bible through craft work and song.

Group size

Up to twelve children with one adult.

What you need

A model Noah's ark with animals, songs about Noah, for example 'Who built the ark?', 'The animals went in two by two', a version of the story of Noah and his Ark, for example the Bible Society's edition, large cereal boxes to make into masks, paint in suitable colours for animals, PVA adhesive, house-painting brushes (3cm to 5cm width), wool for manes, junk oddments.

Preparation

You will need a box for each child. Help the children cut out eyes and a mouth in the right positions to make a mask.

With the children mix the paints and add about one tenth the amount of PVA to the mixture. This will make the paint stick to shiny cereal packets. If you wish, you could also add a small amount of sand to make a textured paint.

What to do

Gather the children together on your carpet area. Show them the Noah's Ark. Read the story and sing some of the songs together. Then show the children the animals. Pick out an individual animal and ask a child to find the other to make a pair.

Move to your painting area and let each child choose a prepared cereal box and decide which animal's face they want to make. Encourage the children to paint and decorate their mask to make their chosen animal.

Discussion

Why did God want Noah to build an ark? How many of each animal went into the ark? How did they know when it was time to come out? What did God send as a promise to the world?

Follow-up activities

✧ Use the masks to act out the story of Noah's Ark to another group of children.
✧ Put the masks in the role-play corner. Provide a large box to be used as an ark.
✧ Using animal stamps to print with, let the children make a picture of the animals going into the ark.
✧ Draw pairs of animals using the photocopiable sheet on page 93.

CHICKEN LICKEN

Objective

English (Reading) – To learn about rhyming words.

Group size

Up to eight children.

What you need

The story of *Chicken Licken* (Ladybird Well-loved Tales edition), a soft toy chicken (optional).

Preparation

Consider the names of the children in your group, and think up some nonsense-rhymes for them, yourself and other adult helpers.

What to do

Read the story of *Chicken Licken* to the children. Use the soft toy as 'Chicken Licken' himself, and ask different members of the group to stand up and pretend to be 'Henny Penny', 'Goosey Loosey', and the other characters. Young children can just stand while you read the story, others may want to speak, particularly if they already know the story well.

Tell the group the name you have thought up for yourself and ask them if they can think up a rhyme for their own name. Most of the second names in the story begin with 'L', so try this sound for everyone first. For example: Jenny Lenny; Winston Linston; Mumtaz Lumtaz; MaiLing Liling.

Occasionally a child may not like his/her name to be used in this way. If so, ask the children to find rhymes for your name, or even for items around them, such as Chairy Lairy and Cupboard Lubord.

Discussion

After they have heard the story, ask the children was the sky falling on Chicken Licken's head? What really happened? What would a horse be called in the story? A cow? A pig? A sheep?

Follow-up activities

✧ Write a group-story based on the Chicken Licken story featuring the children's rhyming names. Put the story together in the form of a book and leave it out for the children to look through.
✧ Record the story on to cassette tape so that the children can listen to it while reading the book.
✧ Draw or cut out pictures of rhyming objects, such as a pan and a man. Mount these on cards and let the children find the rhyming pairs.

THE SUN AND THE WIND

. . . .

Objective

Science — To learn how to keep a drink warm.

Group size

Up to ten children.

What you need

A copy of the story *The Sun and the Wind* (a traditional tale found in many anthologies), warm clothing (coat, scarf, gloves, woolly hat), wrappings of cotton wool, felt and bubble-pack for three similar plastic containers of water, gold card for the sun, blue and white crepe paper for the wind, two pieces of dowel each about 30cm long, adhesive tape.

Preparation

Cut a large circle from the gold card and attach it to one of the pieces of dowel to represent the sun.

Cut strips of blue and white crepe paper twice as long as the stick and attach them to the stick at the top to represent the wind. Fill the three containers with hand-hot water.

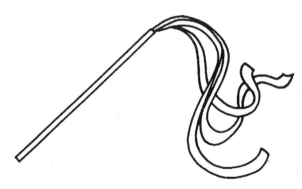

What to do

Dress one of the children in the warm clothing. Read the story of the argument between the sun and the wind about which was stronger. When the sun speaks in the story, hold up the sun and wave the wind when it speaks. Ask them to tell you how the traveller kept himself warm when the wind blew (he wrapped himself in warm clothes).

Let the children feel the plastic containers with the warm water in them. Ask them how they think the water in the containers can be kept warm.

Explain to the children that you want to find out which material keeps the water warm best. Let the children wrap each container in the insulating material, and leave them for an hour. After an hour, feel each container again. Which container do they think is the warmest?

Discussion

Which material worked best? Can any child think why this is? Talk to the children about how we need to dress up warmly if we're going on a journey. What sort of clothes would they want to wear when they are cold? What sort of food do they want to eat? How do they feel when they are hot?

Follow-up activities

✧ Try to cool the containers down when they are heated. Use ice, water and sand to see which works best in an hour.

✧ Ask the children to draw a picture of the traveller when the wind blew, and another of the traveller when the sun shone.

THE MAGIC CARPET

Objective

English — To make up a story with a beginning, a middle and an end.

Group size

Up to ten children.

What you need

A piece of card which can be folded into three (one for each child), lots of crayons, felt-tipped pens, feathers, braid and sequins, A5 card, paper, adhesive sticks. A copy of the story of Aladdin which mentions a magic carpet (such as Disney version).

Preparation

Decorate one of the A5 cards to look like a magic carpet, using concentric rectangles for the carpet pattern, and fringing at each end.

What to do

Read aloud the story of Aladdin, in which a boy finds a magic lamp which contains a genie. He also finds a magic carpet which will take him anywhere he would like to go.

Give the children a piece of A5 card each and ask them to decorate it to make their own magic carpet. Show them the one you have prepared earlier.

Using the three-sided cards, ask the children to draw on the left-hand side the place they would start their imaginary journey, on the middle section they should draw a place they flew over, and on the last side the place they arrived at.

The children now have their own individual theatre with scenery which they can use to tell their story. With older children encourage them to write a sentence for each part of the journey, which can be stuck to the top or bottom of the card, making a simple fold-out book.

Discussion

Where did you go on your magic carpet? Why? Did anyone choose to go somewhere that doesn't really exist? Why? What did you do there?

Follow-up activities

✧ Put an old rug in the role-play area. Decorate it with sequins and tinsel, and let the children pretend to fly off on it. You could decorate the role-play area to look like Aladdin's Cave, with old necklaces and gold-card coins.

✧ Ask the children about other journeys they could imagine that would be magic. What about a magic bus, or a train, or a magic bicycle?

✧ Read *Chitty Chitty Bang Bang*, Ian Fleming (Collins) to the children.

WIGGLY WORM LOOKS FOR A HOME

Objective

Design and Technology — To make a book with a character that moves from page to page.

Group size

Up to six children.

What you need

Ladybird moves home by Richard Fowler (Doubleday), paper, colouring materials, scissors, card cut into 2cm circles, thick wool, PVA adhesive.

Preparation

Cut wool into 20cm lengths, one piece for each child. Make a sample page of your own, with a slit for the 'worm' to slide through. Stick a small card circle on to the end of the wool, to feed it through the slit more easily. Draw a smiling face on the circle.

What to do

Read the book to your group. A card ladybird is tucked into the front cover, which can slide through slits in the pages, looking for a home as you read the story. Point out how the illustrations make it look as if the ladybird has crawled under a leaf and come out on the other side into a different place.

Show the children the page you have made. Show them how you made the slit in the paper and threaded your worm through it.

Put the card circles and the felt-tipped pens on the table, and ask the children to each draw a worm's face on a circle. Give each child a length of wool, and show them all how to stick the circle to the wool (dip the worm's tail into the glue to stop it unravelling). Ask the children to use a piece of paper each and to design a page for their worm to crawl through. Once the pages are finished to their satisfaction, bind each one together to make a group book.

Discussion

Talk about the book they have made. What is their favourite page of the book? Why? What are worms like? Has anyone ever held a real worm? What were they doing at the time?

Follow-up activities

◇ Write down the children's words to tell the story. These could then be cut up and stuck on the appropriate pages of the book.
◇ Set up a wormery to show the children where worms like to live.
◇ Do some worm-like movements, wriggling through hoops, in and out of cones and over and under benches.

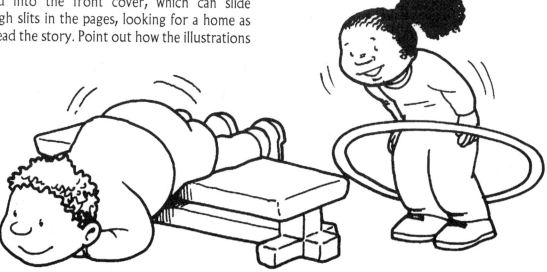

THE MAGI

Objective

Religious Education – To learn about the story of the journey of the Three Kings.

Group size

Up to twelve children.

What you need

A Christmas nativity scene, stiff paper or card strips which will fit around a child's head, glitter, sequins, shiny buttons, scraps of foil etc, *Caspar and the Star* by Francesca Bosca (Lion Publishing), felt-tipped pens or crayons, adhesive sticks, a decorated box with a lid suitable for holding presents for the new King.

Preparation

Start by retelling the Christmas story to be sure the children remember it. Sort your shiny materials by colour into trays or boxes. Cut one side of the card strips into zigzag patterns so that they look like crowns.

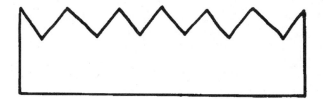

What to do

Read the story of Caspar's journey where he follows a star to meet with the other Magi to search for the special child who will be a king.

Ask the children if they know how we can tell if someone is a king.

Give the children a strip of card each and ask them to colour them with felt-tipped pens and to decorate them with glitter and sequins to look like a crown. Fit each child's crown to their head and fasten together with adhesive-stick.

Ask the children what gift they would like to take to the baby Jesus. Let the children draw the present they would like to give. Put the decorated box next to the nativity scene and the children can place their picture gifts there at any time.

Discussion

What were the three gifts the kings gave? What presents do the children like to get? Who do they give presents to? What nice things could they do which would make a good present for someone they know? Would anyone they know like them to tidy their room without being asked, for example? Why would that be a good present?

Follow-up activities

◇ Put the crowns and some cloaks into the role-play area along with decorative gift-containers. Decorate the cot to look like a crib.
◇ Make a large collage of the Three Kings, using brocades and other rich materials.

THE OWL AND THE PUSSYCAT

Objective

Maths — To put the events of a story in time order / sequencing.

Group size

Eight to ten children.

What you need

The Owl and the Pussycat by Edward Lear (Picture Puffin), photocopiable page 94, scissors, adhesive sticks, pencils and paper.

Preparation

Photocopy enough copies of page 94, one for each child (keep some spares in case of mistakes!).

Read the poem to the children several times through on different days before you do this activity, to familiarise them with the sequence of the story. They may be able to join in the words of the poem after a few read-throughs.

What to do

Read the poem once again, pointing out the illustrations which also tell the story. Give the children a photocopied sheet each and ask them to choose and cut out three pictures which will tell the story of the Owl and the Pussycat. Emphasise that the story must have a beginning, a middle and an end. Older children can then try to write a phrase under each picture to tell their version of what's happening in the story.

Discussion

Ask the children about the poem. Which part of it did they like best? Which is the funniest part? Do they think it really happened? Why?

Follow-up activities

✧ Can the children make a Bong tree or a runcible spoon from Plasticine?
✧ Act out the poem, making up actions for all the verses.
✧ Make a group picture of the characters in the poem, drawing an outline and letting the children fill in the bodies with coloured paper torn from colour supplements or magazines.

CHAPTER 4
MOVING PEOPLE

Activities to find out how we move ourselves around including different forms of transport, how people used to travel and how people using wheelchairs move from place to place are included in this chapter.

MOVING OURSELVES

Objective

PE – To journey from one place to another in the same room, in different ways, using all parts of the body.

Group size

Groups of eight children with one adult helper per group.

What you need

A large area in which the children can move about freely, four large posters/pictures of countries, real or imaginary (for example, pictures of Spain, Greece, Canada and Australia), Blu-Tack to stick the posters to a wall.

Preparation

Stick one poster to each of the four walls of your room at child height. Children should change into loose clothing (ideally shorts and T-shirt) and gym shoes or bare feet.

What to do

Start by asking your group to spread out in the room. Ask the children to sit down. Wait until they have all done so and tell them to stand up again,

then sit down several times. Young children really enjoy this, and it is also a useful warm-up activity.

Ask the children to sit down again, and to stay sitting this time. Point out your four colourful pictures. Now ask them if they can move on their bottoms towards 'Spain'. When they have all done so ask them to move towards 'Canada' lying on their tummies. Continue by moving towards 'Greece' on their backs. You can repeat these actions but backwards. Other ways of travelling are: on knees (forwards/backwards/sideways); squatting (forwards/backwards/twirling around); standing (hopping/jumping/tiptoeing/marching/stamping); any of these with hands in the air/held out to the sides/on heads/on knees or on hips.

Discussion

Which way of moving did they like best? Why? Can they think of any more ways? Why do we have to change our clothes for PE? Ask the children if they know why they need to exercise.

Follow-up activities

◇ Ask the children to paint a picture of themselves doing their favourite action in PE. Display the drawings where you do PE.
◇ Make up some new words to 'Here we go round the mulberry bush', using the children's favourite actions from PE.
◇ Using a timer, measure a minute to see how many times the children manage to hop or jump.

HOW DO WE GET THERE?

Objective

Science – To compare different forms of transport.

Group size

Six children.

What you need

Toys which are forms of transport, ideally a toy bus, aeroplane, car, boat, bicycle, rocket, motorbike and side-car, or a tractor.

Preparation

Think of a list of suitable destinations for a journey, such as: the shops/supermarket (using a bus/car/bicycle/motorbike); a tropical island (boat); Disneyland (aeroplane/boat); the middle of a muddy field (tractor/4-wheel drive vehicle); the moon (rocket).

What to do

Put all the toy vehicles in a line. Suggest a destination and ask the children how they would get there using one of the vehicles. Now ask them to pick up the one they would use and say why they would use that one rather than any other.

Discussion

Talk with the children about the differences between the vehicles. Could you go to the shops in a boat? Is something the same about all the vehicles which run on land? What has wheels, and what has not?

Follow-up activities

✧ Ask the children to draw a picture of how you could get to the moon on a bike, or go to the shops in a boat!

✧ Find some stories about journeys in a variety of vehicles to read to the class and to have a discussion about.

✧ Using each toy vehicle, measure how far they travel when pushed along the floor from a marked point. Which one travels furthest?

GOING BY TRAIN

Objective

History – To find out how people used to travel.

Group size

Six to eight children.

What you need

Pictures of steam-trains, such as the ones found in the large *Thomas the Tank-Engine* picture books by W. Awdry, (Heinemann), a *Thomas the Tank-Engine* colouring book, crayons, a toy railway with an engine and coaches, Lego people or similar.

Preparation

Ideally take your group for a ride on a steam-train (if there is one running in your area) to introduce the idea of travel in the past. Cut up the colouring book so that each child has a sheet to colour. Set up your toy railway.

What to do

Talk to the children about how people used to travel over long distances before there were cars and buses. Show them the pictures of trains, and explain that these special trains used steam, not petrol or electricity. Explain that trains used to be very important to allow people to travel to different places.

Using the Lego people show how the people would get into the trains and be carried to their destinations. Let the children develop this play for a while together.

Now ask them to choose a picture to colour. Talk about their choice. What colour are they going to colour their trains? Why?

Discussion

Ask the children if they have ever travelled on a train. Was it a steam train? Do they know what sort of noise a steam train makes? What sort of a train was Thomas? What were his friends' names?

Follow-up activities

✧ Use some musical instruments to make sound-effects of a train journey.
✧ Put out your toy railway and let the children play freely with it.
✧ Read some of the 'Thomas' stories.
✧ Read the story ' The train who was afraid of the dark' in the resources section on page 77.

A DAY TRIP

Objective

Art — To develop observational drawing, by drawing or painting a picture of something seen on a journey.

Group size

Up to eight children to one adult.

What you need

Clip-boards and pads of unlined paper; charcoal pencils and fine drawing pencils, a pencil sharpener (essential!), old picture frames (without glass) or frames cut from cardboard.

Preparation

Organise a day out for your group. This could be a journey by foot to the local park, or a more complicated outing using public or hired transport. Make sure that there are enough clip-boards and pads for everyone, including yourself and any other adult helpers.

What to do

Explain to the children that you are all going to look around you very carefully to find things which are interesting to draw. The children will find this easier if you give them some ideas. If you are going to a wild-bird sanctuary, the birds could be your subjects. A walk in the park in Autumn could focus on trees and fallen leaves.

Emphasise that the children should draw exactly what they see, including the details of textures and patterns. Show the children how to stand still and sketch a quick outline of something that you see while walking along a path, and then sit on a bench and do a more detailed drawing. By joining in the activity yourself you are showing the children that you think it is important and worthwhile.

When you get back to your base, frame the sketches and hang them on the wall. Invite parents and other members of the community to come and see your exhibition.

Discussion

What did the children enjoy most about their day-trip? What sorts of things were easy to draw? Which things were difficult? Which drawing did they like best?

Follow-up activities

✧ Make a collection of objects the children would like to draw. Put them on a table. Leave drawing materials out on the table, so that the children can go and draw at intervals during the day.
✧ Ask the children to design a clip-board which has places on it for everything they needed when they were on their day-trip.
✧ Ask the children to give titles to their pictures. Make a catalogue for your exhibition using their new titles.

MOVING HOUSE

Objective

Maths – To sort and match furniture to be moved from one area to another.

Group size

Six to eight children.

What you need

A house-corner (with furniture), another area where the 'new house' can be set up, boxes and cartons for packing things into, sheets of paper and black felt-tipped pens, toy prams or trolleys for transporting furniture.

Preparation

Prepare labels for the cartons using the paper and the felt-tipped pens. Put 'plates, cups, knives and forks' on one label, 'pans' on another, 'dolls clothes' on another and so on. Get a new area ready to become the house-corner.

What to do

Explain to the children that they are going to move house with all the equipment from the house corner. Some children can pack away the small equipment into the cartons, while the others move the furniture over to the new house using the prams and trolleys.

Ask the children to clear a pathway from the old house to the new, so that the removal can go smoothly.

Once all the transportation has been done, the next job is to unpack all the cartons and put everything where it is accessible. Take the opportunity of the move to ensure that all items are stored in a way that enables the children to tidy away easily after playing. Draw coloured outlines to show where cups, plates, cutlery, pans and kitchen utensils are stored.

Discussion

Ask the children if they have ever moved house. Who carried all the furniture? How did it get to their new house? How far away was their new house? Did they play with the same children afterwards? Why not?

Follow-up activities

✧ Play 'Kim's Game', using six items from the house on a tray. Let the children look at the tray and ask them to remember what is on it. Cover the tray and remove one item secretly, then ask the children to decide what is missing.
✧ Hold a 'house-warming party' in the new home-corner.
✧ Read *Moving Molly* by Shirley Hughes (Julia MacRae), which is a popular story all about moving to a new house.

VISITING RELATIVES

* *

Objective

Geography — To find out what journeys the children take to see relatives. To explore the idea of places that are far away.

Group size

Any size of group.

What you need

Photographs of some of the children's relatives (if available), paper and felt-tipped pens, a large Child's Atlas, maps of Great Britain and of the world, and red self-adhesive dots (optional).

Preparation

Collect photographs of the children's relatives who live a long distance away. Ask the children how they travel when visiting relatives, and find out the names of the places where these relatives live.

What to do

Look at the atlas together. Explain that if relatives live near you, it takes only a short time to go to visit them, but if they live far away it takes a longer time. Talk about the places the children go to. Are they close to home or far away?

Ask them: if Imran visits his family in Pakistan by plane, how long does it take him to get there? Is it far away, or nearby? If Clancy visits her family in London by car, how long does the journey take? Is it far away or nearby?

Using the photographs (if available) encourage the children to draw pictures of their relatives and to write the names of the places where they live underneath. The pictures could then be displayed on the wall around a map of the world or the country with red dots showing places where the children have relatives.

Discussion

Talk about the relatives the children visit. Are they old or young? Can you play with them? What sort of things do you do at their house? Do you have special food? Point out the things that are different and the things which are the same about the children's experiences of visiting relatives.

Follow-up activities

✧ Ask the children to make a model of the form of transport they use to visit their relatives.
✧ Tell a story into a cassette-recorder about a special journey to see relatives, perhaps for a wedding or a party.
✧ Read the story *Beware of the Aunts!* by Pat Thomson (Picturemac).

Aunty Clare
Brazil

WHEELCHAIR JOURNEYS

Objective

Design and Technology – To find out if it is easy to get about in a wheelchair.

Group size

Four or five children.

What you need

A child-sized wheelchair would be ideal, otherwise a pushchair which will take a child. A short route which includes some steps or ramps. Prams and pushchairs.

Preparation

Make a note of the route you will take, ensuring that there are some areas where it is very difficult, if not impossible to get to if you are in a wheelchair. Set up an obstacle course in your outdoor-play area, or indoors if you have room.

What to do

Introduce the topic by talking to the children about their legs. How do they think they would feel if they wouldn't work? Ask them to pretend that their legs don't work and will not move. Let them take turns sitting in the pushchair/wheelchair while you all play 'Ring-a-roses'. Could they join in with all the actions?

Take the children out for a walk with the pushchair/wheelchair and point out all the places which are difficult to get to if you are disabled.

When you get back to your base, let the children push their prams around your obstacle course, pretending that the dolls are disabled.

Discussion

What could we do to help people who are in a wheelchair? What do they need? How does it make you feel inside when you can't get where you want to go (even when you're just pretending to be in a wheelchair)?

Follow-up activities

✧ Look around you. What things have been done specially to help people in wheelchairs move about? What needs to be done?
✧ Introduce a disabled doll into your role-play area (see page 96 in the resources section for stockists).
✧ Can the children think of other disabilities which would make it difficult to move around?

GOING FOR A WALK

Objective

Music – To listen to a rhyme and match sounds to actions.

Group size

Up to ten children.

What you need

Enough simple percussion instruments for each child to have one, felt-tipped pens, A4 white card.

Preparation

Together with the children, match the sounds you can produce with the words of the story:
✧ Today I decided to go for a walk.
✧ Walked down the garden path (slapping on concrete) – woodblock
✧ Opened the gate (creak) – guiro
✧ And shut it behind me (slam) – clap two books together
✧ Over the short grass (quiet thudding) – tambour
✧ Through the long grass (swish swish) – wire brush on cymbal
✧ Through the sticky mud (squishy noises) – kazoo
✧ Down to the riverbank
✧ Looked up the river (scale going up) – xylophone
✧ Looked down the river (scale going down) – xylophone
✧ Jumped in and swam across (watery noises) – glockenspiel
✧ Climbed a mountain (panting) – voice
✧ Found a cave (eerie noises) – triangle
✧ And there was a lion (roaring) – drum
✧ So I ran down the mountain (all the actions above in reverse, ending with 'And then I was safe').

What to do

Ask the children to play their instrument. What does the sound make them think of? Ask them to draw a picture of what the sound means to them. Use these drawings as cue cards, holding them up at the appropriate moment for that particular sound, just in the way that formal manuscript is used by musicians.

Then take the children through their musical journey to the cave and back. Repeat this several times. Once the children know the words by heart, encourage them to speak it aloud as a group too.

Discussion

Ask the children if they go out for walks with their family. What sort of places do they walk to? Where is their favourite place to walk to? Do they like walking? Why / why not?

Follow-up activities

✧ Ask the children to think of actions to go with the story. It can then be used as an alternative to moving to music in a movement session – movement to choral voice.
✧ Ask the children to draw a map of this journey, starting at a house with a garden, going to the cave and back.

CHAPTER 5
TRANSPORTING OBJECTS

Unusual journeys by water through pipes and Father Christmas down the chimney make some interesting activities to try out.

ACROSS THE RIVER

Objective

Science — To transport a model-animal across water, using a force of some kind.

Group size

Four children at a time.

What you need

A plastic bath or water-tray for a pretend river, blue food-colouring to make the water slightly opaque (optional), model animals from the toy farm/zoo, a plastic box, lid or possibly some plastic boats of different shapes and sizes, aprons, card or stiff paper, scissors, string or cord, Blu-tack, straws, adhesive tape, wooden beads (cubes) which will take a straw through the middle, *Across the Stream* by Mirra Ginsburg (Picture Puffin).

Preparation

Move the bath/tray into place while it is empty. Fill it with lukewarm water, and if you wish add some blue food-colouring.

What to do

Make sure the children are wearing their aprons, and they are fastened securely. Read the story *Across the Stream* by Mirra Ginsburg to the children.

Ask the children how they could get some of the plastic animals, in a boat, across the water to the other side. Can they think of different ways to propel the boat? Experiment with pushing, pulling, blowing and making waves. See if they can improve their boat by adding a sail. Show them how to anchor a bead in Plasticine and put a straw into the hole to use as a mast.

Discussion

Talk about what happened to the plastic animal if the waves got too high, or the children pushed their boats too hard. How many animals could be safely carried across the river? What happened if too many animals were put in the boat? What shape of boat travelled fastest? What shape of boat held the most animals safely?

Follow-up activities

✧ Can the children design and make a boat that will float from paper?
✧ Draw some boat-shapes with chalk on your outside play area. How many children can fit inside the shapes?
✧ Do some maths by placing some plastic animals on card outlines of boats. Place a cow in one boat, a pig in another and two hens in a third — ask the children: how many animals altogether?
✧ Ask them to make up some sums of their own.

WHERE DOES OUR FOOD COME FROM?

Objective

Geography – To discover which countries food comes from and talk about the journeys the food makes.

Group size

Up to twelve children at a time.

What you need

Plenty of tins and packets, some full and some empty, a world map, felt-tipped pens, pieces of paper, one for each country, to make a list of where foods come from, a large sheet of paper to pin up on the wall.

Preparation

Make sure all empty packets are clean, and remove labels from empty tins.

What to do

Look together at the labels and packets. Sort them into piles according to their countries of origin. See if the children can locate each country on the world map. Talk about the long journey the food has made, and show the children how far the journeys are on the map. Compare the length of these journeys to trips which the children may have made on holiday.

Next let the children copy the words describing the contents of the tins and packets onto a list for the relevant country.

Make a large rough outline of the world map. Working in pairs give the children labels and empty packets of produce from one specific country. Tear or cut out the writing from each label into small pieces and stick it onto the map as near as possible to the country it has come from. Stick the lists in the children's own writing on or around the map.

Discussion

Can anyone remember one of the other lands where our food comes from? How do you think it got to our shop? What can we grow in our country? What is your favourite food? Where does it come from?

Follow-up activities

✧ Sort labels into piles according to colour. Cut out the illustrations on them and make a red, yellow or green group picture about food.
✧ Ask the children to design a label for a tin or packet of their favourite food.
✧ Arrange a visit to your local supermarket and ask staff there where the tinned and packeted food originally comes from. You may like to buy the ingredients to make a dish from another country.

FATHER CHRISTMAS' JOURNEY

Objective

Maths — To use flat and solid shapes to make a simple pop-up Father Christmas.

Group size

Six children.

What you need

Small cuboid boxes (individual cereal boxes), patterned self-adhesive plastic, cotton wool, red paper, white paper circles about 6cm in diameter, thick card, PVA adhesive, glitter. Provide five empty containers to put these items in. A version of Father Christmas' journey in story form, for example *Father Christmas* by Raymond Briggs (Picture Puffin).

Preparation

Take the lids off the small cereal boxes, but leave the bases intact. Cut the thick card into strips of about 2cm wide and 15cm long. Cut out triangles from the red paper, to fit on top of the white-paper circle face. Cut 6cm squares from the red paper too. Put all the materials separately in the containers. Make up an example of the Father Christmas to show the children.

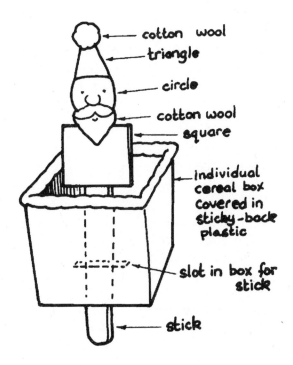

cotton wool
triangle
circle
cotton wool
square
individual cereal box covered in sticky-back plastic
slot in box for stick
stick

What to do

Read the story of Father Christmas to the children.

Now tell the children that they are going to make their own Father Christmas figure. Start by showing the children the things they will use to make their figures and introduce the names of the shapes to the children. To begin, cut a slit in the bottom of a cereal box big enough for a cardboard strip to slide through easily. Cover the box with the plastic and stick cotton-wool around the open edge. Draw a face onto a circle and stick it onto the end of the strip of card.

Stick a square underneath for a body, and a triangle on the head as a hat. Add a cotton-wool beard, dab with adhesive and sprinkle with glitter and the pop-up Father Christmas is complete. As the children are working emphasise the names of the shapes whenever possible.

Discussion

Talk about Christmas night. How do they think Father Christmas carries all the toys? How does he find his way? How does he get into their houses? Ask them about the shapes they used to make their model. Why did a circle make a good face and a triangle a good hat? What do we call the shape of the chimney?

Follow-up activities

✧ Use a simple shape-matching program on the computer for example 'Young Start'(see page 96).
✧ Cut out flat shapes of circles, squares, triangles and rectangles of different sizes from card to make pictures.
✧ Look around your base for shapes made in the environment by windows, door knobs and shelves and talk about the different shapes we can see.

MAKING A BAG

Objective

Design and Technology – To design and make a bag to carry a currant bun.

Group size

Six to eight children.

What you need

Different types of paper, for example newspaper/wrapping paper, cake cases, string or cord for handles, adhesive, adhesive tape, red felt-tipped pens. Examples of paper carrier bags. 'Currant buns', baker's hat and some pennies.

Preparation

Make some imitation currant buns using a piece of crumpled tissue stuck into a cake-case with a blob of red felt-tipped pen stuck on the top. Alternatively use toy buns or even bake currant buns with the children to use for this activity.

What to do

Elect one child to take a turn as the shopper and one as the baker. Sing/say the rhyme together:
'Five currant buns in a Baker's shop,
Big and round with a cherry on the top,
Along came *Ahmed* with a penny one day,
(substitute the child's own name)
Bought a currant bun and took it right away.'

   Let one child buy a currant bun from the baker.

   Explain that the children are each going to make a bag in order to carry their buns safely home. Show them the examples you have and explain how they are made.

Let the children try to make a bag using the different kinds of paper you have available. Ask them to tell you what they are choosing to use, and why. Ask them to test their bags to see if they will carry their buns.

Discussion

Ask the children about the bag they have made. What was it made from? What did they use to stick it together? What happened to your bun? Ask the children where they go to get cakes and buns.

Follow-up activities

✧ Set up a baker's shop in the role-play area, with white aprons and hats. Put some coloured salt-dough and pastry cutters in the shop and let the children make pretend buns.
✧ Use the cakes to do some addition and subtraction. Ask the children to give one doll two cakes and then another one. How many altogether? How many would be left if you took two cakes away?
✧ Organise a visit to your local baker's shop to see 'behind the scenes'.

THE JOURNEY OF WATER

Objective

Design and Technology — To find out how water gets to our homes.

Group size

Up to twelve children.

What you need

A sink, a toilet, a washing machine (optional), paper to draw on, felt-tipped pens/crayons.

Preparation

Ensure that the children can all see into the sink. Check that you can remove your toilet cistern lid. Pull your washing machine forward slightly so that the hoses can be easily seen.

What to do

Ask the children if they know where water comes from and how it gets to our houses. They may have already learned something about this on television.

Take the children to the sink and tell them about the pipes that carry the water to the tap, and how the water is cleaned so that we can drink it. Point out the drain, where the water goes away. Move on to the washing machine (if available) and talk about what we use it for. Show them the hoses which bring the clean water in and take the dirty water away. Go to look at the toilet. Look inside the cistern and see the water filling it. Look at the pipes which take the dirty water away.

Ask the children to draw a picture of one of the above, showing the clean water coming in, and the dirty water going out.

Discussion

Ask the children what they know about the journey the water takes to their home. What is it like when it comes in? What is it like after it has been used? What does it travel in? Where does the water in the reservoirs come from? What would we do if there wasn't any water? Introduce the idea that we must not waste water.

Follow-up activities

✧ Set up some water-play in the sink, with hoses so that the effects of siphoning water to make it move can be explored.
✧ Using a child's bucket, let the children fill a paddling pool in the summer. Does it take a long time? What would make it easier?
✧ Put a container outside to catch the rain. Measure how much falls in a period of one week.

THE JOURNEY OF A SEED

Objective

Science — To discover some of the ways seeds journey away from their parent plant.

Group size

Six children.

What you need

Places where the children can see and collect various seeds which transport themselves in different ways. For example: 'helicopters' — sycamore seeds/lime seeds; 'parachutes' — dandelions/rosebay willow herb; 'explosives' — balsam pods/shepherd's purse; 'stickers' — burdock/goosegrass. A bag to carry the seeds in, pots in which to sort the different seeds, a book to stick seeds into, adhesive tape or adhesive, pencils, a magnifying glass.

Preparation

Walk around your area to find out where the various plants are growing, and plan a route for your group to follow.

What to do

Take the children to collect the different types of seeds. Back at your base sort them into sets and look carefully at each type of seed you have collected, encouraging the children to look through the magnifying glass and tell you what they see.

Ask the children to stick the seeds into the book, one type on each page. They can then try to draw the seeds next to them on the page, making them much larger than they are, as they saw them through the magnifying glass. If they want to try, encourage them to write the names of the plants underneath their drawings.

Discussion

Ask the children what the seeds felt like, and what they looked like. Did they notice anything more when they used the magnifying glass? What happens if you plant a seed? Why would it help a seed to grow away from the plant it grew on?

Follow-up activities

✧ Collect lots of seeds and make pictures by sticking them onto sheets of paper. Brush with PVA adhesive diluted with a little water for a glaze. This technique can also be used to decorate boxes to hold Harvest gifts.
✧ Plant some seeds in pots. Plant some very crowded together and some well spaced out. Which ones will grow best?
✧ Make a weighing-area with various seeds to weigh and some scales for the children to play with.

WHEEL PATTERNS

Objective

Art – To make a journey across a piece of paper using a toy car with wheels dipped in paint.

Group size

Four to six children.

What you need

A bicycle and a doll's pram, toy cars with different patterns and sizes of tyres. One car for each colour paint you are going to use. Large sheets of paper, paint in assorted colours, plastic saucers or shallow trays.

Preparation

Mix paint if necessary. Cover all surfaces in paper to protect your tables. Put one toy car with each saucer of paint. (Each saucer should have a different colour of paint in it). Start with four colours and add more as the children become more confident.

What to do

Take your group outside on a wet day. Push the bicycle and the pram through the puddles. Look at the tracks they leave behind. Back inside, encourage the children to dip the tyres of one of the cars in the paint and run it over the paper to make a coloured track. Repeat this with the other cars/colours. Remind the children to replace the car they are using in its saucer before picking up a different one.

Ask the children to 'drive' their cars all over their paper. Once they have experimented with the cars, ask the children to select just two or three colours and make a pattern with them.

Discussion

Ask the children about their patterns. What colours did they use? What happened to the paint on the tyres? What happened to their fingers?

Follow-up

✧ Ask the children to choose other toys to make patterns to print with. Railway track, the rims of plastic cups or doll's feet make interesting tracks.
✧ Dip marbles or beads in paint and roll them backwards and forwards across the paper placed at the bottom of a plastic tray with sides.
✧ Use a white candle to draw hidden patterns on white paper. Let the children discover the picture by painting in thin coloured paint on the page to disclose the wax. Can they make a surprise picture for their friends?

PAPER AEROPLANES

Objective

Science – To make a paper aeroplane which will fly.

Group size

Up to ten children.

What you need

Farily stiff paper, paper–clips, a small mat from which to launch the planes. Markers of some kind to show how far the children's planes have travelled.

Preparation

Decide where you are going to test your paper aeroplanes and clear away any obstructions, so that the planes can fly uninterrupted. Cut the newspaper up into pieces measuring 20cm by 20cm and the same size as the stiff paper.

What to do

Practise folding paper with the children. Start using newspaper and encourage the children to fold them into aeroplanes. First fold the paper in half lengthwise, then fold down two corners to make a point, finally fold these in half to make a dart.

Talk to the children while they are folding, to make sure that they understand what to do.

Then give each child a piece of stiff paper and ask them to make a paper aeroplane from it. Give each child a paper-clip to put on the nose of their plane. Once they have done this, take turns to throw the aeroplanes from the mat, and see which one flies furthest, marking the spot with the name of the child who made the plane. Repeat this a few times, until it is clear which plane flies furthest. Paint the aeroplanes and throw them again.

Discussion

Talk about the paper aeroplanes. Was it hard to make a plane? Whose plane flew furthest? What effect did the painting have on the way the aeroplane flew? Has anyone ever travelled in a real aeroplane? What keeps a real aeroplane up in the air?

Follow-up activities

✧ Use these folding skills to make some other simple items such as a paper hat, or a paper boat.
✧ Make a pop-up card by folding paper and sticking it inside a card. Decorate the paper to look like an aeroplane.
✧ See who can throw a ball, a quoit, a bean bag the furthest. Try different types of throw.

CHAPTER 6
FINDING THE WAY

In this chapter children can use geography skills to follow a treasure trail and language skills to talk about how they feel if they cannot find the way home.

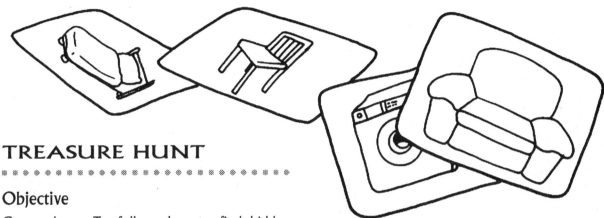

TREASURE HUNT

Objective

Geography – To follow clues to find hidden treasure.

Group size

Four to eight children.

What you need

Small cards about the size of a playing-card which can be easily hidden, a black felt-tipped pen, 'Treasure' – gold foil chocolate coins are ideal.

Preparation

Make a clue-card for each child. These can be drawings of things in the room, under or behind which you have hidden the next clue.

The last clue will lead to the treasure, which should be something which can be shared by all your treasure seekers.

Hide the clue-cards in their places around the room, all except the first one, which you will give to the first child.

What to do

Explain to the children that they are going to have a treasure hunt, and that they will have to guess where to find the next clue.

Hand the first clue to the first child. As the child tries to find the next clue give help by saying 'getting warmer' or 'getting colder' to direct the child to the clue. When the first child finds a clue the next child can take a turn and so on. When the treasure is finally found, share it out so that everyone can enjoy it.

Discussion

Have the children ever found hidden treasure? What did they like best about the game? What things do they have which are precious to them? Why? What treasure would they like to find?

Follow-up activities

✧ Read a story about treasure, such as *The Treasure Sock*, Gollancz 'Share-a-Story' series.
✧ Draw maps of a treasure-island showing where the treasure is buried. Ask the children how they would hide the map.
✧ Make a collection of beads, coins and gold-coloured items and put them in a treasure-chest made from a shoe-box decorated with shiny paper. Put it in the role-play corner for the children to make up their own stories about treasure while playing with it.

NUMBER JOURNEYS

Objective

Maths — To follow a sequence of numbers in the correct order.

Group size

Between eight and twelve children.

What you need

Space for the children to move freely. Set of cards with numbers 1 to 10 written on. Blu-tack, coloured pencils in a variety of colours.

Preparation

Fix the numbered cards up on the wall. Start with numbers one to five at first, to establish the concept that numbers follow each other in a certain order. Put the card with '1' near the door where the children enter, then put the other numbers at roughly equal intervals around the room in order. Write the numbers one to ten randomly on a sheet of paper and photocopy enough for your group.

What to do

Explain to the children that you want them to move around the room in a group and to stand near the numbers as they are counted out loud.

Encourage the children to count with you, but insist that they do not say a number until they are close to it. Point out that number one always comes first and is followed by number two, and that they have to move in the correct order to count correctly.

When you return to your working area, encourage the children to collect their own copies of the photocopiable sheets and coloured pencils. Ask the children to draw a coloured 'road' from number one to the other numbers in the correct order. When they have done this, ask them to do it again in different colours so that they end up with a rainbow-coloured 'road' linking their numbers in the correct order.

Follow-up activities

✧ Punch holes on the number-cards and thread ribbon through them. Have an equal number of dolls, fluffy toys etc. and show the children how to put them in a line with '1' at the beginning and '10' at the end.

✧ Cut doors in the sides of five shoe-boxes. Put the boxes on the floor and number them one to five on top of the boxes. Stick matching numbers onto toy cars, scatter the boxes around on a playmat, and show the children how they can 'drive' the cars into their matching garage as part of their play.

SHAPE STEPPING-STONES

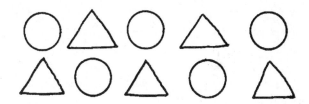

Objective

Maths – To recognise and follow a trail of geometric shapes.

Group size

Between six and eight children.

What you need

Sheets of brightly-coloured A2 card or strong paper in at least two colours, an open area of carpet or corridor where the children can move freely.

Preparation

Choose two geometric shapes which you would like your group to learn about for example: circle and triangle. Cut out 20cm circles from the coloured card, producing as many as you can fit on the sheet. Cut triangles of the same size from the other coloured sheet.

Cut any other shapes you choose from different coloured card or paper. If your children are capable of doing it themselves, let them cut out their own shapes.

What to do

Show the children the shapes and ask them if they know what they are called.

Place the circles on the floor in a line, and put the triangles next to them. Ask the children to walk along a row of one of the shapes, using them as stepping–stones. When you are sure that the children know these shapes, mix up the two lines together, making sure that it is still possible to get from one shape to the next similar one in one step. Can the children hop along the stepping–stones? Can they jump along them?

Discussion

Talk about what your chosen shapes look like. Which shapes have corners? Which are round? What shape would you see if you looked at bricks in a wall? Which shape has three points on it? Talk about the game you have played. How did the children know where to step next? Which was easier, walking or hopping?

Follow-up activities

✧ Use other shapes instead of triangles and circles. Add a third and a fourth shape as the children get better at following the trail.

✧ Paint shape-trails on the surface of your outdoor play area and let the children make up their own games, such as shouting the names of shapes out for other children to follow.

✧ Lay a trail of shapes into different areas of your building, then go on a 'square', 'circle' or 'triangle' walk, stepping on the correct shape to take you to a large shape stuck onto a door or a wall.

LOST

* *

Objective

English – To explore how we feel when we are lost.

Group size

Six to ten children.

What you need

A copy of the story of *Hansel and Gretel*, scrap paper / scrap material or a ball of string, a route for a short walk preferably indoors.

Preparation

Cut the paper or material up into scraps (if you are using this), or make sure that the string is long enough to cover the route on which you will take the children.

What to do

Read the story of *Hansel and Gretel* to the children. Can the children remember how Hansel found the way back to his home the first time they were lost? Explain that you are all going to go for a walk, carefully leaving a trail behind you, to see if you can all find the way back easily just as if you were in a real forest.

Go for your walk, letting the children take turns at dropping the trail or unwinding the string. When you have reached the end let the children take turns at picking up the trail or winding the string. Make it a rule that whoever is doing this is the leader, and no-one else must go in front of them, otherwise some children will run straight back to base leaving all the work to the others!

Discussion

Have any of the group ever been lost? How did they feel? What can we do to find the way home if we are lost? Who are the people we could ask for help?

Follow-up activities

✧ Use the photocopiable master sheet on page 89 to find a way through the trees to get from house-to-house.
✧ Help the children learn their addresses. Explain that this will help them if they ever do get lost.
✧ Paint a picture about being lost. What colours would they want to use?

ON THE ROAD

Objective

English — To learn to understand instructions.

Group size

Any size of group.

What you need

The photocopiable sheet on page 95, adhesive-sticks, scissors, and felt-tipped pens.

Preparation

Photocopy enough copies of the sheet on page 95 for each child to have one and a few spares.

What to do

Look at the photocopiable sheet together. Point out the road which runs through the picture, and explain to the children that they are going to cut out the vehicles at the bottom and stick them on the picture one at a time. Explain that they must listen carefully to what you are going to tell them about where they should place the vehicles.

Very young children can try to cut the rectangles out. Older or more able children can try to cut around the outline of the vehicles.

Talk about the pictures on the page, making sure that the children can identify each picture.

Ask the children to cut out and stick the items one at a time, waiting while they do it. For example tell them to:
✧ Put the police car on the road outside the paper-shop.
✧ Put the fire engine on the road leading to the house.
✧ Put the bicycle next to the duckpond.
✧ Put the train on the railway track.
✧ Put the bus on the road near the bus-stop.
✧ Put the car on the road going past the church.

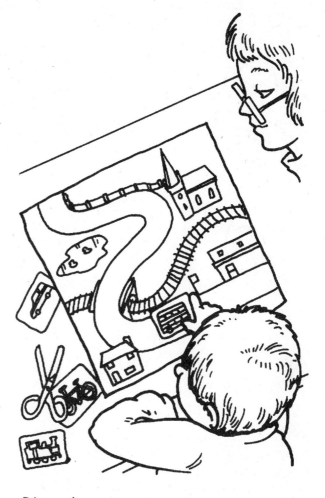

Discussion

Ask the children to show you where they placed the vehicles on their picture. Why do they think the fire-engine is going to the house? Why is the car going past the church?

Follow-up activities

✧ Ask the children to tell you a story about the people in the vehicles. Write the words for them and let them copy your writing, or encourage them to try the writing themselves.
✧ Using a play-mat do the same activity using animals from the zoo or farm. Can the children put them in the right place?
✧ Make a 3D model of a street and use toy cars to park next to, in front of, alongside etc.

A JOURNEY USING TOUCH

Objective

Science — To think about how much we need our eyes to move about freely.

Group size

Ten children.

What you need

A scarf to use as a blindfold, a room with furniture placed around it. Some braille paper, any stories you can find about our senses, in particular, touch. The poem 'Feeling the way' on page 67.

Preparation

Arrange the room so that the furniture provides obstacles. Check that none of the children will get upset if they wear the blindfold.

What to do

Ask the children if they can walk across the room without banging into the furniture. Let them show you that they can. Then ask them if they could still do it if they couldn't see. Give everyone a chance to wear a blindfold and see if they can get across the room safely using their hands to help them. If any child does not want to wear a blindfold, ask them to walk across the room with their eyes closed instead.

Talk about our senses with the children, invite the children to feel the braille paper — what do they think it is for? Read the poem to the children.

Discussion

Ask the children how did it feel when you couldn't see where you were going? What would it be like to be blind? What other things would it be difficult to do? Is there anything a blind person can't do at all? What can a blind person use to help themselves?

Follow-up activities

✧ Put some everyday items into a cardboard box with a hole in the lid. Let the children put their hand into the box and feel an item. Can they guess what it is without seeing it?
✧ Use a touch-matching game such as Galt's tactile button matching game (see page 96).
✧ Make a set of cards with rectangles of different colours and textures of material on them (velvet, denim, floral cotton etc.). Choose one card and describe it without showing it to the children. Can they pick it out? Once the children can do this, let them take turns to describe a card for the other children to recognise.
✧ Make a 'feely' picture using different materials.

WALKING THROUGH THE JUNGLE

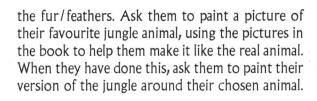

Objective

Science — To look at the features of the exotic animals which live in the jungle.

Group size

Any size of group.

What you need

The poem 'Walking through the jungle' on page 74, pictures of animals likely to be found in the jungle including snakes, monkeys, crocodiles and parrots. Books about jungle animals, including books borrowed from your local library children's department. Paint and paper, aprons.

Preparation

Read the poem to the children, encouraging them to answer you by making the noises of the animals.

What to do

Ask the children if they can find a picture of their favourite jungle animal in the books. Give each child a piece of paper with the name of their favourite animal written on it. Show them how to use an index to find some information about their animal in the book.

Ask the children to look carefully at the pictures of jungle animals — look at the colours on the fur/feathers. Ask them to paint a picture of their favourite jungle animal, using the pictures in the book to help them make it like the real animal. When they have done this, ask them to paint their version of the jungle around their chosen animal.

Discussion

Do we find parrots and monkeys in our countryside? Where might we find them in this country? What is different about the places where they still live wild? Are there lots of places like this left in the world? What can we do to help these animals?

Follow-up activities

◇ Read the book *A Nice Walk in the Jungle* by Nan Bodsworth (Picture Puffin).

◇ Make some sound effects to accompany the poem ('Walking through the jungle') using any instruments you can make. Sandpaper on two blocks rubbed together makes a really good hiss for a snake for example.

◇ Make a list of the things you would need if you went walking through the jungle. Would you need a fur coat? What sort of shoes would you need?

TWINKLE TWINKLE LITTLE STAR

Objective

Science – To look at why we need light in the dark.

Group size

Six to eight children.

What you need

A torch, a place which has no daylight, or a table big enough to crawl underneath with your group and a blanket or throwover thick enough to exclude most of the daylight.

Preparation

Make sure the children know all of 'Twinkle Twinkle Little Star' including the third verse:
'Then the traveller in the dark
Thanks you for your tiny spark
He could not see where to go
If you did not twinkle so.'

Cover the table with the blanket. Check that it will be dark enough for the torch to be seen. Check the torch batteries are working.

What to do

Sing 'Twinkle Twinkle Little Star' with the children. Explain that this song was written at a time when there were no lights on the roads, and people had to travel in the dark, by moonlight and starlight.

Tell the children that you are all going to play a game to see how you feel in the dark, and whether we feel better with a light on. Crawl under the blanket with your children and sing 'Twinkle Twinkle Little Star' again, switching the torch on and off at intervals, whenever the words of the song suggest darkness.

Discussion

How did the children feel when they were in the dark? Would they like to travel a long way in the dark with no lights on the road? What might happen? How do we feel when there are bright lights around us? Which do they prefer?

Follow-up

✧ Make some bright shiny stars using collage materials like foil and sequins and tinsel. Display them on a dark background of black paper.
✧ Read some stories about day and night such as, *Bears in the Night* by S & J. Berenstain (Collins).
✧ Make a collection of things we use to provide light, such as candles and lamps. Display them on a table with labels saying what they are.

CHAPTER 7
DISPLAYS

A good display will show off children's work in an interesting and attractive way.
Familiar and unusual approaches can be used to create visual appeal.

IDEAS FOR DISPLAY

Backgrounds

Choosing the right background is important for setting the tone for the whole display.

Wrapping paper is a cheap and attractive alternative as a background for children's work; stripes in particular give a professional look. Newspaper is even cheaper and is excellent as a background to a display with examples of the children's own news.

Whatever paper you have available can be made more colourful if the children paint it, let them spatter a suitable colour or combination of colours over sheets of your chosen paper. Alternatively the children could put random patches of adhesive on the sheets and gently sprinkle powder-paint or sand onto the patches.

Scribbled finger-painting also makes a very good background for displaying children's work. This can be done on newspaper, brown wrapping paper, wallpaper, or whatever else you have available.

Silhouettes

Use a large silhouette in a relevant shape to mount work onto. For a display on the topic of 'Journeys', mount the children's work on a large silhouette of a bus, a boat, a train or a plane.

Pictures of the children's favourite holidays could be mounted on a huge postcard or a suitcase for example. Cut out the silhouette shapes from plain or patterned paper, card, material or even corrugated plastic.

Frames

Displays look neater and more attractive with a frame around them. A strip of contrasting coloured paper or fabric around the edge looks effective for a whole-wall display. Wrapping paper cut into strips makes a bright and cheerful frame. Individual children's drawings or paintings look impressive if they are fastened into an empty picture frame (without glass) using adhesive tape or Blu-tack. Mounting children's work on pieces of contrasting card or paper also looks effective.

ACTIVITIES

59

Using texture

Add interest to your displays using different materials. Add sand and adhesive to paint to make a rough textured effect. This is particularly useful in yellow paint for a display about a journey to the seaside for example.

Textured fabrics make good backgrounds to children's work, and can be used together for contrasting effects, try hessian and brocade for example. For a display about a journey in space, mount the children's pictures on black velvet.

Corrugated card (used for packing goods) makes a wonderful textured backing to displays. For a display on 'Journeys' ask the children to cut out shapes such as wheels from pieces of this card and display them on the card, twisting the corrugations slightly in relation to the backing, the result will be a display which looks like an optical illusion.

Interactive displays

Children love books which pop up or move in some way, and your displays can use this feature by providing opportunities to lift flaps and move parts. Hide names or photographs under the flaps to show who painted the picture. A display using a map could have animals or products belonging to each country hidden under the flaps. A display of children's postcards could lift up to show a photograph of the child who wrote it.

3D displays

There are many ways of creating displays which have three dimensions, which have depth as well as height and breadth.

Boxes of all kinds can be used to make 3D displays. They can be used to make effective boats, steam engines, cars or buses, which are firmly attached to the display board, or they can be used to mount a picture. Folded and curled paper makes an excellent 'jungle', and animal heads made by the children can then be mounted on small boxes to make them stick out.

Children's work

In an early-years environment children's drawings and paintings should form the main part of any display. Decide whether to leave children's work on their original rectangles of paper, or experiment by offering the children paper cut into different shapes which are suitable for the topic of journeys, to see if this influences their choice of subject. Paintings should be mounted carefully, sometimes by cutting them along their contours rather than leaving them in their original paper shape.

It is often very effective to mix children's work with published material, such as prints of famous paintings of journeys, postcards and posters.

Lettering

Lettering on a display should be appropriate, and easily read. Large letters can be easily cut out from gummed paper in different colours to suit the theme of the display. Hologrammatic paper or card makes very eye-catching lettering for displays, as does wrapping paper and corrugated card. Patterned self-adhesive plastic can be cut into letter-shapes and stuck straight onto the display. This can be particularly useful if the pattern used echoes the theme, for example plastic decorated with a *Thomas the Tank Engine* scene for the topic of 'Journeys'.

Lettering within displays should always be neatly printed on a label. Consider putting a border around these labels, or using 'clouds' to give them extra definition.

SPACE TRAVEL

What you need

Black or dark blue velvet to cover the display board, a staple-gun or drawing pins. Alternatively, get the children to paint some textured wallpaper with black and dark blue paint. One empty plastic washing-up liquid bottle between each two children, crêpe paper, adhesive tape or stick, felt-tipped pens, sequins, glitter, kitchen foil, stiff card.

Preparation

Prepare the display board (cover in fabric or paint). Cut the plastic bottles in half lengthways. Cut the rocket fins from card.

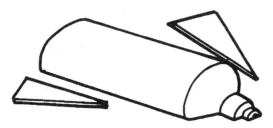

What to do

Ask the children to each cover their half of a bottle with kitchen foil. The card fins need to be decorated with felt-tipped pens, and can then be stuck to the back of the half-bottle.

Strips of crêpe paper in different colours can be fixed to the bottom of the rocket.

Stick sequins, glitter or pieces of foil onto the display board to look like stars. Staple the rockets to the board by their fins and cut out the letters of the words 'Space Travel' from kitchen foil.

Discussion

Has anyone ever seen a rocket? Where did they see it? Has anyone ever seen a film with a rocket in it? Who operates rockets? Where do they go? Who would like to go on a journey in a rocket? Where would you go?

WHO WROTE THIS?

What you need

Postcards written by your group from a real or imaginary holiday. (See the photocopiable sheet on page 91 and Send a postcard on page 20). A photograph of each child in your group, adhesive tape or sticky labels about 15cm wide, pencils, felt-tipped pens, a staple-gun or drawing pins. Large sheets of white paper.

Preparation

Fix the sheets of white paper to the display board and draw a shape to represent the back of a postcard, with a stamp on it as a background.

What to do

Attach the photographs of your group to the board. Make a hinge with the adhesive tape or sticky label, and attach each child's postcard to the board in such a way that it can be lifted up like a flap above their photographs. Cut letters or write a label saying 'Who wrote this?' and attach this heading to the top of the display. Invite parents and children to read what is on the postcard and guess which child wrote it.

Discussion

Has anyone ever sent a postcard? Who did they send it to? Why did they send it? Who wrote the message? Do the children know which postcard on the wall belongs to which child? How do they know?

CHAPTER 8
ASSEMBLIES

This chapter gives ideas for assemblies or group sharing times based on the theme of Journeys. Children can be given opportunities to reflect on how we can make journeys to explore new places and to visit old friends.

TRAVELLING IN DIFFERENT WAYS

The focus for this approach is on different forms of transport.

The assembly involves the children in drawing on experiences they may have already had during other activities, across the curriculum, for example in movement sessions.

These activities should have informed them about the variety of ways in which people may travel, even if perhaps their destinations may sometimes be the same.

This assembly should lay the foundations for a future understanding of how the same goals may be achieved in a range of ways, depending on each individual person.

Introduction

Begin by inviting the children to recall all the different modes of transport which they have learned about in their practical work. These could be listed on a flip chart, or displayed in the form of pictures, posters, models, toys, slides or OHP transparencies. When the selection is completed, draw attention to the enormous diversity reflected in it.

Some children could present the results of data handling work which shows the various ways in which they travel to school/nursery/playgroup or perhaps their favourite modes of transport.

Activity

A group of children should present a pre-planned role play or drama in which various people are all trying to reach the same destination but each one by a different route and mode of transport.

Someone may choose to travel by air, because it is quick. Another person may like to travel by bicycle, because it avoids traffic jams and provides excellent exercise, but another may feel that a car is more comfortable, especially in the rain!

At the end of the drama, all the people should have arrived at the final destination, (at different times) expressing satisfaction with the mode of transport they chose to use.

Reflection

Encourage the children to reflect on why people may choose to travel in different ways; because of their different interests and needs. Consider how, in the end, they will all reach the same destination in what is the best way for them.

Prayer

Some children may wish to thank God for all the different forms of transport across the world and those people who are connected with them.

Song

The song *Trains and boats and 'planes* provides a suitable conclusion; or the children could sing some songs they have learned about transport.

TAKING A JOURNEY

The focus for this approach is on the school/nursery/playgroup outing.

This may be an outing to a place of interest, such as a park, a museum or the seaside. Whatever the destination may be, it is probably true to say that for many young children, the journey is often as exciting as the place itself — this is especially the case when the form of transport used is one with which the children are not particularly familiar!

Although you will probably want to emphasise the enjoyment to be gained from group outings, you can also make sure children are fully aware of safety requirements linked with journeys and travel of all kinds.

Introduction

Begin by reminding all the children of their recent outing or journey. This may be done in a variety of ways; perhaps a display of photographs, postcards, guidebooks and other souvenirs could be created in the assembly area or children may be able to talk about where they went and what they did there. Drawings, paintings and models commemorating the visit could be shown by the children who produced them.

Activity

Invite the children who travelled on the journey to re-create it in a drama or role play.

The re-enactment should begin with details of the preparations that were necessary; these might include some discussion of the arrangements that had to be made, the clothes that had to be worn and an example of the kinds of food and drink that could be brought.

Then ask the children to describe the transport they used, the route which they took and to relate what they saw and experienced on the journey itself. It may be appropriate to mention any particular incidents which occurred, such as the songs that were sung on the coach, or the train which broke down!

If it is relevant, the return journey could also feature as an element in the drama.

Reflection

Invite the children to spend a few moments in silence, so that they can think about all their memories of the journey and how they felt about it. If it is possible, it would be useful to show colour slides taken on the journey to help focus the attention of the children at this point.

Prayer

Some children may wish to thank God for the opportunities which they have to travel and to ask that they may always return safely.

Song

The words of a well-known favourite like *The wheels on the bus* can be easily adapted to reflect particular experiences; the children may also like to sing some of the songs which they enjoyed on the journey itself.

SPECIAL PLACES

• •

The focus for this approach is on journeys to special places.

Many young children will look forward to even the most long and tedious journey if their final destination is one which they long to reach; a visit to a theme park, the seaside or the home of a relative may involve long hours of travelling, but all the effort will be thought worthwhile once they have finally arrived!

In many religious traditions, pilgrimage is seen as a particularly important kind of journey and places such as Jerusalem, Lourdes and Mecca attract huge numbers of visitors each year. If any of the children have direct experience of pilgrimage, then it might be appropriate to include these in the assembly, in addition to an exploration of other special places.

Introduction

Begin by asking the children to think of places where journeys begin — their homes, railway stations, bus garages, airports for example.

These could be listed on a flip chart or recorded in pictorial form or the children could show toys, drawings, paintings or models which show their suggestions.

A graph could also be displayed, showing which destinations are the most popular with the children, or perhaps one which reveals the places which they would most like to visit if they had the opportunity to do so.

Activity

Some children would present a pre-prepared role play, showing a group of travellers with different destinations.

The role play could be set in an airport, a railway station or perhaps a port and the children should be dressed to represent various kinds of travellers, complete with luggage and other props appropriate to their destinations.

Each child should tell the others where s/he is planning to go and why that place is so special as to warrant a long and perhaps difficult journey. This section of the assembly should therefore use the ideas which the children have suggested themselves during discussion activities.

If there is enough time, additional 'scenes' could be included in which the children show what happens at their chosen destinations.

Reflection

The children should be invited to spend a few quiet moments in thinking about places which are special and important to them and why; it may be appropriate to link this part of the assembly with some of the examples given in the role play.

Prayer

Some children may want to thank God for the special places in their lives and to ask for the opportunity to return to them soon.

Song

A song which links with the destinations selected by the children would be particularly relevant here, such as *Going to see my Granny* or *We're all going on a summer holiday.*

Collective worship in schools

The assemblies outlined here are suitable for use with children in nurseries and playgroups, but would need to be adapted for use with pupils at registered schools. As a result of legislation enacted in 1944, 1988 and 1993, there are now specific points to be observed when developing a programme of Collective Acts of Worship in a school.

Further guidance will be available from your local SACRE — Standing Advisory Council for RE.

POEMS AND ACTION RHYMES

FEELING THE WAY

(Awareness of the visually-impaired)

The way to Grandma's is
wriggly straight wriggly straight
The way to Grandma's is
bumpy smooth bumpy smooth
The way to Grandma's is
prickly rough prickly rough
Lane,
pavement,
footpath,
bridge,
And then I'm at Grandma's.

'I can see you're happy today,' she says
'I can see you're happy today.'
But I have to trace her smile with
my fingers
And feel her crinkly eyelines
Before I can say the same thing
about her.

Jan Jones

Notes

This poem is designed to make people think about journeys from different points of view. For instance how does a walk to the local shop 'feel' to your feet or your fingers?

'Feeling the way' deals with touch and orientation and the effect the road surface has on this particular visually-impaired child (is she in a pushchair or is she walking, I wonder?). Can the children listening to the poem describe the 'sound' of their journeys to school or the 'smell' of various landmarks along the way? How would they describe the feel of their journeys? Is it possible for a small group to map out an entire route using no visual clues at all? (for example, turn left at the smell of the bakery, turn right when the railings go round a corner; straight on until you hear the noise of the playground, etc.).

PHOTOCOPIABLE RESOURCES

A GOOD PLAY

We built a ship upon the stairs
All made of the back-bedroom chairs,
And filled it full of sofa pillows
To go a-sailing on the billows.

We took a saw and several nails,
And water in the nursery pails;
And Tom said, 'Let us also take
An apple and a slice of cake';
Which was enough for Tom and me
To go a-sailing on, till tea.

We sailed along for days and days,
And had the very best of plays;
But Tom fell out and hurt his knee,
So there was no one left but me.

Robert Louis Stevenson

WHERE ARE YOU GOING, JENNY?

Where are you going Jenny,
Dressed in green?

I'm going to the palace
To dine with the Queen.

Where are you going, Jenny,
Dressed in red?

I'm going for a ride
On Santa's sled.

Where are you going, Jenny,
Dressed in blue?

I'm going to have tea
With a kangaroo.

Where are you going, Jenny,
Dressed in white?

I'm going for a sail
On the ship of the night.

John Foster

TRAVELLING

How far to school?
Not far by car.
How far to the sea?
Not far for me.
How far home again?
Not far by train.
How far to Spain?
Not far by plane.
How far to the shop?
Not far if you hop.
How far from here?
To where my dear?

Jan Pollard

PHOTOCOPIABLE RESOURCES

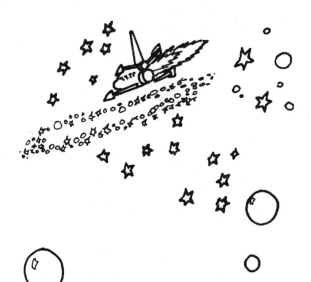

THE SOLAR SYSTEM TOUR

Climb aboard! Yes, climb aboard!
You'll have a lifetime's thrill.
You'll *love* the Solar System Tour.
We know,
we *know* you will!

We'll whizz you right round Saturn,
then Mercury, then Mars.
See Venus, and see Neptune.
You'll spot
a million stars!

Jupiter and Uranus!
Pluto! Our Earth and Moon!
So, climb aboard the spaceship.
Be quick!
We're leaving soon!

Wes Magee

SITTING IN MY BATH-TUB

Sitting in my bath-tub,
I have sailed the seven seas.
I have anchored by the taps.
I've been shipwrecked off the knees.

I have sailed into the unknown
To beat off an attack
From a fleet of pirates lurking
Round behind my back.

I have sailed between the fingers
Where no other ship has been
I've explored the murky depths
In a soapy submarine.

Sitting in my bath-tub,
I have sailed the seven seas.
I have anchored by the taps
I've been shipwrecked off the knees.

John Foster

UP THE WOODEN HILL

Up the wooden hill to bed
thumb in mouth, you sleepy head,

one step,
two steps,
hold my hand,

three steps,
four,

that sandy man
will sprinkle dreams into your eyes
and fly with you through rainbow skies,

five steps,
six,

half way — half way

up the wooden hill to bed
thumb in mouth, you sleepy head,

seven steps
eight steps
twirl a curl

nine steps,
ten,

the moon's a pearl
glowing through a milky mist
to give a drowsy night-time kiss,

eleven steps,
twelve,

this is the way

up the wooden hill to bed
thumb in mouth, you sleepy head.

Gina Douthwaite

UP THE STREET YOU GO

Up the street
and down the street
and up the street you go.
Walking the dog,
walking the dog,
up the street you go.

But wait a minute,
wait a minute,
surely that's not true.
Look who's pulling,
pulling, pulling!
The dog is walking *you!*

Wes Magee

MAGIC CARPET RIDE

Let's pretend our rug by the fire
is a magic carpet ride.
We can fly up into the sky,
we can soar, we can skim, we can glide.

We can swoop down over our house
and make everybody jump.
We can take off into the air
then fall back down with a bump.

We can fly out over the ocean
pay visits to foreign lands.
We can dine with Queens and Kings,
build castles on golden sands.

And if we're really tired
or feeling sad and alone,
we'll climb aboard our carpet
and set a course for home.

Brian Moses

THE DOUBLE-DECKER BUS

We like, riding on the double-decker bus.
Up on the top-deck that's the place for us!

In the front seat with the driver down below,
We give the orders, tell him where to go.

Tell him when to speed up, when to slow down.
We drive the double-decker right through the town.

We drive it up the hill and park by the gate.
We make sure that the bus is never late.

We like riding on the double-decker bus.
The front seat on the top deck —
That's the place for us!

John Foster

GOING PLACES

A Jumbo is an elephant,
it also is a plane.
They both take people far away
and bring them back again.

A joey is a kangaroo
inside a furry pouch.
His mother leaps around with him,
OUCH! OUCH! OUCH!

Cygnets are baby swans,
and swim by mother's side,
and then they climb into her back
and she gives them a ride.

Mum's car is called a Beetle,
the inside seats are black.
She drives us everywhere in it
and *we* sit in the back.

Jan Pollard

I SAW A SHIP

I saw a ship a-sailing
A-sailing on the sea;
And, oh! It was all laden
With pretty things for me!

There were comfits in the cabin,
And apples in the hold;
The sails were made of silk,
And the masts were made of gold.

The four-and-twenty sailors
That stood between the decks,
Were four-and-twenty white mice
With chains about their necks.

The captain was a duck,
With a packet on his back;
And when the ship began to move,
The captain said, 'Quack! Quack!'

Traditional

MINIBEAST MOVEMENTS

This is the way
the beetle stumbles,
clumsy, clockwork, slow.

This is the way
the grasshopper leaps,
so, so, so!

This is the way
the snail slides,
smooth, steady, sure.

And this is the way
the spider scuttles
swiftly across the floor.

Tony Mitton

ROUND AND ROUND THE GARDEN

Round and round the garden
Like a teddy bear;
One step,
Two steps,
And tickle me under there!

Round and round the lighthouse
Went the spiral stair;
One step,
Two steps,
Right up in the air!

Round and round the haystack
Like a little mouse;
One step,
Two steps,
In this little house.

Anonymous

WE ARE OFF TO TIMBUCTOO

We are off to Timbuctoo
Would you like to go there, too?
All the way and back again,
You must follow our leader then,
You must follow our leader,
You must follow our leader,
All the way and back again.
You must follow our leader.

*[One person is the leader; the others
follow, copying actions]*

Traditional

WALKING THROUGH THE JUNGLE

Walking through the jungle,
What do you see?
Can you hear a noise?
What could it be?
SSSSSSSsss

Over there!
A snake
looking for his tea.

Creeping through the jungle,
What do you see?
Can you hear a noise?
What could it be?
Grrrrr

Over there!
A tiger
looking for his tea.

Running through the jungle,
What do you see?
Can you hear a noise?
What could it be?
Trump trump

Over there!
An elephant
looking for his tea.

Leaping through the jungle,
What do you see?
Can you hear a noise?
What could it be?
Roarrrr

Over there!
A lion
looking for his tea.

Swinging through the jungle,
What do you see?
Can you hear a noise?
What could it be?
Chitter chatter

Over there!
A monkey
looking for his tea.

Wading through the jungle,
What do you see?
Can you hear a noise?
What could it be?
Snap snap
Snap snap

Over there!
A crocodile
looking for his tea...
hope it isn't me!

Julie Lacombe

STORIES

SING TO THE SWALLOWS!

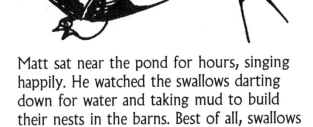

Matt and his dad had just moved a long way to Swallow Farm and Matt was fed up. He didn't want to leave his friends behind.

'You'll make new friends,' promised his dad. 'Wait till you go back to school...'

'That's *ages* away,' thought Matt. 'A whole summer holiday away.'

Matt wandered around the farmyard feeling lonely. He was just wondering whether he could sail a boat on the pond, when something darted past his knee, took a sip of pond water and soared high into the sky. What was happening?

It was a bird! A swallow! Matt recognised it from the picture on the farm sign. Sure enough, streamer-tailed swallows were swooping around all the barns and coming down to drink from the pond as they flew.

These chirping, beautiful birds made Matt want to sing and one day, he made up his own song about the swallows, which he sang to the tune of *Ring a ring o' roses:*

The sky is full of swallows,
The sky is full of swallows,
Swishing, swooping
Flying up and down.

Matt sat near the pond for hours, singing happily. He watched the swallows darting down for water and taking mud to build their nests in the barns. Best of all, swallows nested in the roof above Matt's window — Matt's own swallow family!

In the Autumn, swallows gathered, twittering, on the telephone wires. Matt and his new schoolfriends rushed home from school to see them.

But one afternoon, all was quiet. The wires were empty.

'Where are my swallows?' Matt cried.

'They're on their way home,' said his dad.

'My swallows live *here*!' shouted Matt, crossly.

'Your swallows live here in spring and summer and they have their families. Then they go back to their other home in South Africa for autumn and winter,' Matt's dad explained. 'And now they've started their long journey back. It's called migration.'

All through winter, Matt missed the swallows and he worried about them. He knew how tired he felt after a train trip to London — and these little birds didn't even go by train, but had to *fly* themselves all the way to South Africa!

PHOTOCOPIABLE RESOURCES

Then, one dark evening in March, Matt's dad said, 'Your swallows are leaving the lions behind now. They're coming back, Matt. Look!'

He pinned up a large map on the wall.

'We'll cut out cardboard swallows to stick on and imagine what their journey is like...'

Every night they talked about the swallows flying over the rainforests and the sandy desert. Then across Europe and the mountains of Switzerland. Soon, they would be crossing the channel from France, over the ships...and some would find their way to Swallow Farm!

Now Matt was worried again. He couldn't find his way to his granny's in the next town on his own — so how would the swallows find the farm after their 6,000 mile journey?

'They know where they are by where the sun is,' Matt's dad explained, 'and they look for landmarks and listen for noises they know.'

'I can help!' cried Matt excitedly. 'I'll sing to the swallows! They know my swallow song!'

Matt sang to the swallows every day. He sang while he fed the pigs, he sang while he collected the eggs and he sang while he helped to fetch the cows.

But every day the skies were empty.

Matt became more and more worried. Surely his swallows hadn't lost their way?

Then, one April morning, he saw a black speck in the sky and then another...

'My swallows are back!' cried Matt. 'They heard me!' And he sang his swallow song again and again as two swallows swooped through the gate of Swallow Farm.

Geraldine Taylor

More about migration

Most migration journeys are made between a summer place to breed and a warmer place for winter.

Creatures which migrate include some butterflies, birds, whales and eels.

Many birds journey to Britain to spend the winter here.

More about swallows

Swallows usually complete their journey from South Africa to Britain in six weeks.

Swallows feed on insects, and they arrive in Britain when insects are plentiful.

All over the world, people welcome the arrival of the swallows. In Westphalia many farmers and their families wait by the farm gate for the arrival of the swallows and open the barn doors for them.

In Japan it is believed that swallows bring good fortune and the Chinese used to build special nesting ledges for them.

In Austria there is a legend that swallows helped God to build the sky.

THE TRAIN WHO WAS AFRAID OF THE DARK

In a cosy, wooden shed in the middle of the countryside lived a train. During the daytime he was a very happy, little train.

But at night, the train wasn't happy at all. As soon as it got dark he began to get scared. The little train was frightened of the dark. He knew it was silly, but he couldn't help it.

Every night he would open the door to his shed so that the moonlight could make everything bright. The cold wind made the little train shiver, but he didn't mind. He would rather be cold than frightened.

Early one morning, the little train pulled up at the village station. There were lots of passengers waiting and they all scrambled aboard. They wanted to go into the big town, where most of them worked.

The little train set off on his journey, travelling very gently along the railway track.

CLICKETY-CLACK!

CLICKETY-CLACK!

As he passed the cornfield, the passengers waved to the scarecrow. The scarecrow smiled and waved back.

Suddenly there was a loud SCREECH!

Sparks flew up from the little train's wheels as he skidded to a halt at the entrance to a dark tunnel. The little train hated tunnels.

Inside the tunnel, it was very, very dark.

'I can't go in there,' thought the little train. 'It's probably full of spiders and bats.'

'There might be monsters!' he said. 'Or even ghosts!'

The little train was very, very frightened.

'I'll go a different way to the town,' he decided, and he turned away from the tunnel and sped across the cornfield.

The terrified scarecrow leapt out of the way. And the farmer called out angrily, 'Get out of my cornfield, you naughty little train!'

The ride across the cornfield was a bumpy one and the passengers began bouncing out of their seats.

One old lady was enjoying every minute of it.

'Wheee!' she laughed.

But the rest of the passengers were very unhappy. A little boy's ice-cream cone landed on his dad's nose. And a baby's bottle flew into the air, showering everyone with sticky orange-juice.

'Ugh!' they all shouted.

Having reached the foot of a very tall mountain, the little train began his steep climb to the top.

The passengers gazed silently out of the windows.

'Oh dear!' gasped one terrified lady. 'What a long drop!'

The little train arrived at the top of the mountain and then sped down the other side.

'Too fast! Too fast!' the passengers screamed as hats and bags and umbrellas flew through the carriage windows.

'Wheee!' shouted the old lady.

The little train came to a stream which was crossed by a rickety, wooden bridge.

'I'm not crossing over that!' said a young man. He took off his shoes, rolled up his trousers and paddled across the stream.

As the little train crossed the bridge, it began to shake from side to side. Pieces of wood began to splinter and soon the bridge started to fall apart.

The little train had just managed to reach the other side of the stream when the whole bridge crumbled and tumbled into the water with a loud SPLASH!

The little train then rushed through the park, scattering all the children from their playground.

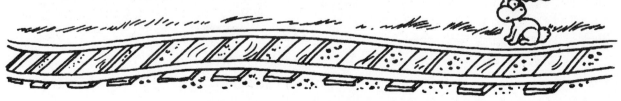

His metal wheels churned up the sand-pit, throwing sand everywhere, which covered all the passengers from head to foot.

Soon, the little train arrived in the town. All the shoppers were horrified to see a train hurtling down their busy high street.

Cars and taxis and buses all screeched to a halt.

The little train had caused a traffic jam and there was a deafening sound as all the drivers sounded their horns.

As soon as they heard the noise, police cars came rushing from the police station.

And fire engines from the fire station.

And that made the traffic jam worse.

Much later, the little train arrived at the station. All the passengers tumbled out of the carriages and hurried to their offices, banks and shops.

'You've made us late for work!' they all shouted, angrily.

At the end of the day, the passengers decided not to travel home on the railway.

Some travelled by ferry-boat.

Some travelled by bus.

Some travelled by taxi and some decided to walk home.

One very rich passenger travelled home by helicopter and as he passed over the station, he shook his fist angrily at the little train. The little train was very upset.

Only one passenger arrived at the station to be taken home by the little train.

It was the old lady.

'I hope this journey is going to be as exciting as this morning's journey,' she laughed.

The little train had caused enough fuss for one day, so he decided to travel home the proper way.

But when he came to the dark tunnel, he couldn't go any further.

'I'm frightened of the dark,' he cried.

'Well, put your lights on, you silly train!' said the old lady.

The little train hadn't thought of doing that! He switched on his lights and he could see right through the tunnel to the opening at the other end.

As he travelled through the tunnel, the little train could see there was nothing to be frightened of.

There were a few spiders.

There were a few bats.

But none of them took any notice of the little train.

'And there are no such things as ghosts!' laughed the old lady as they pulled up at the village station. 'No such things as monsters!'

The old lady had found the journey very dull, but she knew that all the other passengers would have enjoyed it.

The following morning, the village station was crowded with waiting passengers. The old lady had told them all that the little train was no longer frightened of the dark. The little train was very happy to see everyone scramble aboard.

That night the door of the wooden shed was shut tight. The little train switched his lights on. And off.

And on.

And off.

Then he went to sleep. There was nothing to be frightened of.

Denis Bond

EMILY AND THE GOLDEN ACORN

Once upon a time there was a great oak tree.

It had grown through many seasons — spring, summer, autumn and winter — year after year.

The tree stood in a garden, and next to the garden was a house, and in the house lived a little girl. Her name was Emily, and she loved the tree. She knew that in the tree there was magic.

For Emily and her younger brother, Jack, the tree was a pirate ship. The trunk was a mast, the branches were the spars, and the leaves, as they filled with the warm summer breeze, were the sails.

One afternoon, when a fierce wind blew, their dad came out and said, 'I don't think you should be up in that old tree in this weather. It's too dangerous. It might fall down.'

That night, before she went to sleep, Emily looked out of her bedroom window at the old tree and made a wish.

Later, under the full moon, the tree began to change.

The next morning, Emily awoke and looked out of her window. Something had happened. Instead of houses and gardens, there was now a shining sea.

Emily ran to wake Jack, and together they rowed out to where Emily's tree had stood, and where now stood a pirate ship, rigged and ready to sail.

'She's called the *Golden Acorn*,' said Jack.

'Anchors aweigh, Master Jack!' Emily cried, and they set sail across the back gardens and into the street.

'Morning,' said Ted the postman. 'Lovely weather for a sail, but they do say there's a storm brewing.'

They sailed out through the town, past houses, shops, church spires, factory chimneys and hills, until at last they reached the open sea.

They sailed across an ocean as blue as crystal, and a dolphin swam with them, leaping and laughing in the sparkling waves. They saw far-off islands, a whale, and many wonderful things. Then, far away on the horizon, they spied a golden light.

The golden light came from a tiny tree perched on top of a towering black rock. Emily could see dark storm clouds looming all around it.

'Set sail for the light, Master Jack!' Emily cried, but the strong wind was already blowing them there.

As they drew closer to the rock, the ship began to pitch and roll in the heavy seas.

Emily climbed the mainmast, while the wind and sea raged around her. Jack threw the iron anchor to make fast the ship to the black rock.

The *Golden Acorn* heaved in the great swell and, just as the anchor struck the rock, a huge wave crashed against the ship and covered Jack completely.

Emily was sure they had reached the edge of the world. She looked down and saw where the sea fell away to a storming, bottomless chasm!

'The light on the tree is a golden acorn,' Emily yelled against the wind, but there was no reply. There was NO JACK! The wave had swept him away.

Emily picked the golden acorn from the branch.

Its golden light fell over the dark sea. *No Jack!*

She clambered down the mast. *No Jack!*

She rushed to the other side of the ship. *No Jack!*

Suddenly the wind changed. The ship strained against the rope.

If the rope broke, how would she save Jack?

Then above the roar of the storm, she heard a cry: 'Emily! Emily!'

It was Jack, riding on the back of the dolphin!

No sooner had Jack climbed the ladder to safety, than the anchor rope snapped, and the wind began to blow them back, back, back from the edge of the world.

They sailed on until Jack saw a light in the distance. It was their bedroom window. They were nearly home. They waved goodbye to the laughing dolphin. A last great wave flung them into their garden, and the ship came to rest. Emily held on tightly to the golden acorn.

When the weather cleared, they found that the old oak tree had blown down.

Later, Emily gave her dad the golden acorn. 'It's treasure,' she said, 'from the edge of the world.'

'It's a treasure indeed,' said her dad. They planted the acorn where the old tree had stood. Soon a new tree would begin to grow.

(Author's note: The oak tree was consecrated to the god of thunder, because oaks are more likely to be struck by lightning than any other tree.)

Ian Beck

SONGS

JOURNEYS IN YOUR MIND

Catherine Morrell

WHERE DID MY BANANA COME FROM?

Ask the children to think of other types of food that have to make a journey to reach them. Follow the 'food journeys' on a world map.

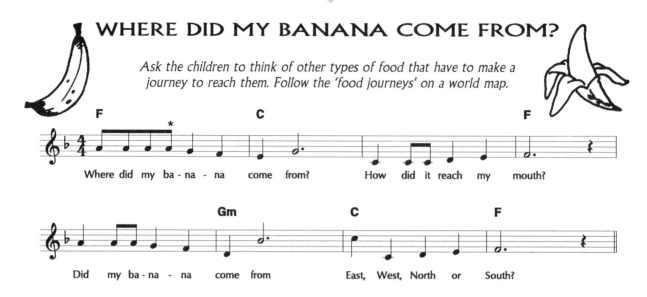

Where did my ba-na-na come from? How did it reach my mouth?

Did my ba-na-na come from East, West, North or South?

Peter Morrell

GO TO TOWN CALYPSO!

1. Now you can go to town___ on a bus, Go with Russ, but go___ on a bus! You

pay your fare___ and soon you're there,___ Go-ing to town___ on a bus.

2. Now you can go to town on a train,
Go with Wayne, but go on a train.
The trees whizz past, you move so fast
Going to town on a train.

3. Now you can go to town on a bike,
Go with Mike, but go on a bike.
You know the road, and your Green Cross Code,
Going to town on a bike.

4. Now you can go to town in a car,
Go with Ma (Pa!), but go in a car.
Go left and right and watch the lights,
Going to town in a car.

Sue Nicholls

PHOTOCOPIABLE RESOURCES

MY LITTLE CAR

Make up some more verses with suggestions from the children: 'Bill's big lorry', 'Dad's/Mum's red Metro' ...

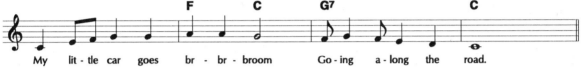

1. My lit-tle car goes br - br - broom, Br - br - broom, br - br - broom,

My lit-tle car goes br - br - broom Go-ing a-long the road.

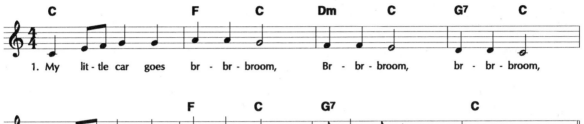

2. My little car goes br br broom,
Slowing down, br br broom.
(singing gradually gets slower)
My little car is standing still
(pause)
Now you can cross the road.
(very distinctly)

3. My little car is off again,
Br br broom, br br broom,
My little car is off again,
Going along the road.
(original speed)

Jean Gilbert

POSTCARD FROM THE SEASIDE

Hav-ing a love-ly time, wish that you were here, Hav-ing a love-ly

time, walk-ing on the pier. Hav-ing a love-ly time, and the weath-er's

fine. I am at the sea-side hav-ing a love-ly time.

Clive Barnwell

THE STEAM TRAIN

Use these 'sound effect' lines as desired e.g. all together, line by line, as a round! Have fun!

When the fire-man's put in his sho-vel of coal and the wat-er's bub-bl-ing hot! When the

steam is read-y to push and pull and the dri-ver's read-y for off! When the

guard has waved his lit-tle red flag and the whis-tle's sound-ed loud. Then it's

time for the wheels to clat-ter and clang and turn a-round and a-round... and the train goes...

Chug-a-chug-a-chug-a-chug-a- chug-a-chug-a-chug-a-chug-a- chug-a-chug-a-chug.

Ooh - eee, ooh - eee, ooh - eee.

Huff and puff, huff and puff, huff and puff.

Shh, shh, shh, shh, shh, shh.

Last time only

Lesley Funge

WE'RE GOING ON A JOURNEY

This is suitable for use as an action song, performing appropriately during the second section of each verse. It could also be used as an 'echo' song, with a leader singing each bar and the children echoing.

1. We're go-ing on a jour-ney, You come too. We're go-ing on a jour-ney to the moon.

Step in-to space-suits, On goes the hel-met, Climb in-to the rock-et, Off we go.

---

2. We're going on a journey
   You come too;
   We're going on a journey
   To the beach.
   Down to the station
   Climb aboard the train then
   Whistle blows, flags wave,
   Off we go.

3. We're going on a journey
   You come too;
   We're going on a journey
   To London Town.
   Down to the garage
   Climb into our car then
   Belts on, close doors,
   Off we go.

4. We're going on a journey
   You come too;
   We're going on a journey
   Through the air.
   Down to the airport,
   Up into the plane then
   Fasten your safety belts,
   Off we go.

5. We're going on a journey
   You come too;
   We're going on a journey
   Into town.
   Down to the bus stop
   Upstairs we clamber
   Sit in the front seats,
   Off we go.

6. We're going on a journey
   You come too;
   We're going on a journey
   On the sea.
   Down to the harbour,
   Board the ferry boat then
   Up goes the gang plank,
   Off we go.

7. We're going on a journey
   You come too;
   We're going on a journey
   On our bikes.
   Pump up the tyres,
   Fasten your helmet,
   Up into the saddle,
   Off we go.

Carole Henderson-Begg

KIDS IN SPACE

1. How would you like to come for a ride in space?
Have-n't you heard it's quite an ex-ci-ting place? We'll leave
it all be-hind, And we will climb up and ex-plore
Where no-one has gone be-fore. 2. And known as the first kids in space.

2. What would you say to spending a day on Mars?
Or we could try to fly to the Moon and stars.
Then home to Earth we'll race,
And we'll be known as the first kids in space.

Debbie Campbell

X IT MARKS THE SPOT!

In the verses, the children can suggest different treasures. The song can last as long as is needed!

Chorus

Search-ing for trea-sure us-ing a trea-sure map. Search-ing for trea-sure, X it marks the spot!

D.C. al Fine

1. Will we find dia-monds deep in a hid-den cave? Will we find dia-monds in a pi-rate's chest?
2. Will we find go-ld deep in a hid-den cave? Will we find go-ld in a pi-rate's chest?

Clive Barnwell

PHOTOCOPIABLE RESOURCES

I WROTE A LETTER TO GRAN

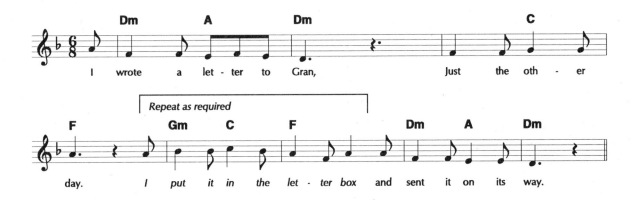

I wrote a letter to Gran, Just the other day. I put it in the letter box and sent it on its way.

Where the song words are in italics you can add an extra line in each verse:

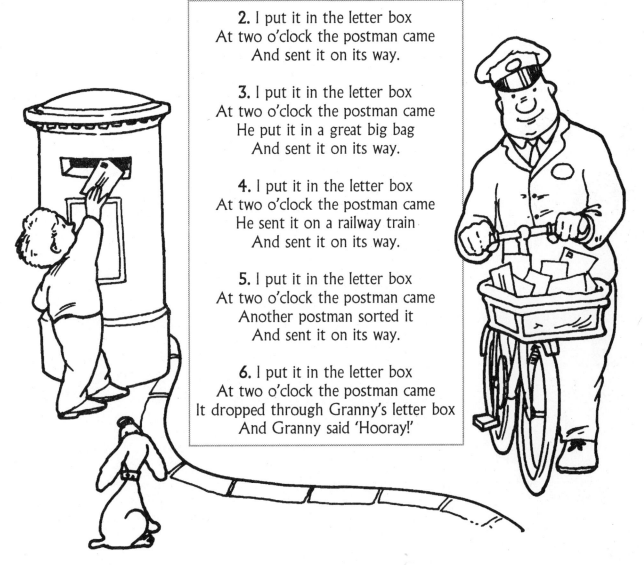

2. I put it in the letter box
At two o'clock the postman came
And sent it on its way.

3. I put it in the letter box
At two o'clock the postman came
He put it in a great big bag
And sent it on its way.

4. I put it in the letter box
At two o'clock the postman came
He sent it on a railway train
And sent it on its way.

5. I put it in the letter box
At two o'clock the postman came
Another postman sorted it
And sent it on its way.

6. I put it in the letter box
At two o'clock the postman came
It dropped through Granny's letter box
And Granny said 'Hooray!'

Jan Holdstock

PHOTOCOPIABLE RESOURCES

THEMES
for early years

Name _____

Our traffic survey

Car	
Bus	
Lorry	
Tractor	
Bicycle	
Fire Engine	
Motorbike	
Other	

THEMES
for early years

Name _____

A path through the woods

THEMES
for early years

Name _____

Dress the dolls

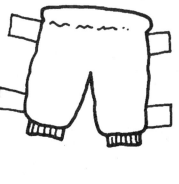

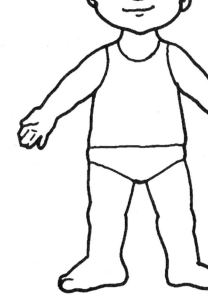

THEMES
for early years

Name _____

Write a postcard

THEMES
for early years

Name _____

The town mouse and the country mouse

The town mouse went

_____

He did not like

_____

The country mouse went

_____

He did not like

_____

THEMES *for early years*

Two by two

Draw each animal a partner to go into the ark.

THEMES
for early years

Name _____

The Owl and the Pussycat

THEMES
for early years

Name _____

On the road

RECOMMENDED MATERIALS

STORY BOOKS
Beware of the Aunts!, Pat Thomson [Picturemac]
Caspar and the Star, Francesca Bosca [Lion]
Chicken Licken, Jonathan Allen [Ladybird Favourite Tales]
Chitty Chitty Bang Bang, Ian Fleming [Collins]
Come for a Ride on the Ghost Train, Colin & Jacqui Hawkins [Walker]
The Day Jake Vacuumed, Simon James [Pan books]
Father Christmas, Raymond Briggs [Picture Puffin]
Gerry's Seaside Journey, Michelle Cartlidge [Little Mammoth]
Hansel and Gretel, Jacob & Wilhelm Grimm [Ladybird Favourite Tales]
Happy Hats, Peter Curry [Hippo]
The Jolly Postman, Allan & Janet Ahlberg [Heinemann]
Ladybird Moves Home, Richard Fowler [Doubleday]
Moving Molly, Shirley Hughes [Julia MacRae]
A Nice Walk in the Jungle, Nan Bodsworth [Picture Puffin]
Noah's Ark, (Bible Society Edition)
Over in the Meadow, Louise Voce [Walker]
The Owl and the Pussycat, Edward Lear [Walker]
Rosie's Walk, Pat Hutchins [Picture Puffin]
The School Trip, Nick Butterworth & Mick Inkpen [Hodder]
The Sun and the Wind, (Traditional)
This is the Bear, Sarah Hayes & Helen Craig [Walker]
The Town Mouse and the Country Mouse, Helen Craig [Walker]
The Treasure Sock, (Gollancz 'Share-a-Story' series)
Wait and See, Tony Bradman [Little Mammoth]
Willow Pattern Story, Allan Drummond [North-South books]
You Can't Catch Me, Annabel Collins [Red Fox]

INFORMATION BOOKS
First Discovery - On Wheels, [Moonlight]
White Rabbit's Colour Book, Alan Baker [Kingfisher]

SONG AND RHYME BOOKS
Action Songs, ill. Wendy Smith (Picture Lions)
Favourite Rhymes, Ronne Randall (Ladybird)
Okki-Tokki-Unga: Action Songs for Children (A & C Black)
Rub-a-Dub-Dub, Val Biro (Blackie & Son Ltd.)
Songs, Scholastic Collections (Scholastic)

OTHER RESOURCES
Lenny the Letter (see page 20)
Resources for teachers about *Lenny the Letter,* including videos, computer disks, talking books, worksheets, colouring sheets and posters are produced by the Post Office. A catalogue 'Educational Resources from the Post Office', listing prices is available from the Post Office Education Service, P O Box 145, Sittingbourne, Kent ME10 1NH (telephone 01795-426465).

Button-matching game (see page 56) and *disabled 'Dara' doll,* (see page 41), available from James Galt & Co. Ltd., Brookfield Road, Cheadle, Cheshire SK8 2PN.

Disabled equipment for dolls (about 38cm high) is available from NES Arnold Ltd., Ludlow Hill Road, West Bridgford, Nottingham, NG2 6HD.

Young Start, shape-matching program, by Douglas Woods, (see page 45).

PHOTOCOPIABLE RESOURCES